Reading
WOMEN'S POETRY

"Laurence Lerner, poet, novelist and critic, offers an enjoyably readable survey of poetry by women, ranging from the famous to the neglected. *Reading Women's Poetry* is engagingly informative, warmly responsive and incisively analytical. Lerner is lucid, provocative and entertaining." CEDRIC WATTS, Research Professor of English at Sussex University, author of many critical books, including *Literature and Money* and *The Deceptive Text*

"Do we read poem X because it's a good poem, or because its revealing of its author's marginalised status? To Laurence Lerner, both are good reasons for reading it, and no harm is done to poetry by attention to matters outside the ordinary scope of critical judgement. Lerner is a born teacher and his book evokes the ideal classroom discussion. He is wonderfully knowledgeable and he reads the poems with insight, skill and enthusiasm, but we are also encouraged to think for ourselves and take pleasure in what we read. *Reading Women's Poetry* is an immensely stimulating book." CLIVE WILMER, Fellow of Sidney Sussex College, Cambridge, and author of *The Mystery of Things*

Reading
WOMEN'S POETRY

LAURENCE LERNER

sussex
ACADEMIC
PRESS

BRIGHTON • PORTLAND

2 4 6 8 10 9 7 5 3 1

First published in 2009 by
SUSSEX ACADEMIC PRESS
PO Box 139
Eastbourne BN24 9BP

and in the United States of America by
SUSSEX ACADEMIC PRESS
920 NE 58th Ave   Suite 300
Portland, Oregon 97213-3786

British Library Cataloguing in Publication Data
A CIP catalogue record for this book is available from the British Library.

Library of Congress Cataloging-in-Publication Data
Lerner, Laurence.
Reading women's poetry / Laurence Lerner.
   p. cm.
Includes bibliographical references and index.
ISBN 978-1-84519-337-9 (acid-free paper) —
ISBN 978-1-84519-334-8 (pbk. : acid-free paper)
1. English poetry—Women authors—History and criticism. 2. American
   poetry—Women authors—History and criticism. 3. Poetry—
   Authorship—Sex differences. I. Title.
PR111.L47 2009
821.009′9287—dc22

                                                              2009002325

Typeset and designed by SAP, Brighton & Eastbourne.
Printed by TJ International, Padstow, Cornwall.
This book is printed on acid-free paper.

Contents

Acknowledgements		vii
Introduction		1
1	The Beginnings	11
2	Augustan & Romantic	25
	Anne Finch	25
	Furious Sappho: Pope and Lady Mary	28
	Vile Dependence: Complaints of Marriage	34
	Women against Slavery: Hannah More	37
	Charlotte Smith	42
	Romanticism & Politics	46
3	The Nineteenth Century	55
	The Breaking Heart: Mrs Hemans and L.E.L.	55
	The Brownings	59
	Marian Erle's Fate Worse than Death	68
	Stealing, Murder, Female Bonding	72
	The Castaway	77
	Emily Brontë	80
	Prepare your Fortitude: George Eliot	86
	Christina Rossetti	91
	Three Radicals	100
	Augusta Webster	100
	Mathilde Blind	104
	Amy Levy	108
	Emily Dickinson	
	The Moon's Dropped Child: Charlotte Mew	123
4	The Twentieth Century	128
	Ecriture Féminine & Modernism: A Note	128

Contents

The Americans	130
Marianne Moore	130
Elizabeth Bishop	139
Two Retellings: H.D. & Denise Levertov	145
Ways of being Modern: Edna St Vincent Millay	152
The Radicalisation of Gwendolyn Brooks?	155
Sylvia Plath	158
The English	164
Elizabeth Daryush	164
Ruth Pitter	166
Kathleen Raine	168
Stevie Smith	171
Aurora Leigh or What is it like to be a woman poet?	177
A Name of One's Own	189
Index	193

Acknowledgements

A Personal Note of Thanks

I am grateful to those friends who read parts of this book and sent me their comments, all of which were helpful and all of which are greatly appreciated, including those I was ungracious enough not to adopt: Molly Mahood, Olga Meidner, Marianne Thormahlen and Werner von Koppenfels.

A Formal Note of Thanks

The author and publisher gratefully acknowledge the following for permission to reproduce copyright material:

Cover illustrations: Lady Mary Wortley Montagu (detail of an oil painting by Sir Godfrey Kneller, 1715; Private Collection); Augusta Webster, née Davies) after Ferrando, © National Portrait Gallery, London.

Textual reproduction: "I Remember" and "The Jungle Husband" from the Collected Poems of Stevie Smith, copyright © 1972 by Stevie Smith. Reprinted by permission of New Directions Publishing Corp.; and Hamish MacGibbon, courtesy of the estate of James MacGibbon;

Lines from "Still Life" by Elizabeth Daryush. Reprinted by permission of Carcenet Press Limited;

Lines from the poetry of Denise Levertov. Reprinted by permission of Pollinger Limited, Authors' Agents;

"I being born a woman and distressed" and "I shall forget you presently". Copyright © 1922, 1923, 1950, 1951 by Edna St. Vincent Millay and Norma Millay Ellis. Reprinted by permission of Elizabeth Barnett, Literary Executor, The Millay Society;

Reading
WOMEN'S POETRY

Introduction

I'm Nobody! Who are you?
Are you – Nobody – Too?
Then there's a pair of us?
Don't tell! They'd advertise – you know!

How dreary – to be – Somebody!
How public – like a Frog –
To tell one's name – the livelong June –
To an admiring Bog!

EMILY DICKINSON

Is this poem about being a woman, in a world which echoes to the noises of the male frogs? Is that the right way to read the poem? Is it *a* right way? No use asking the author, who left no instructions on how to read her poems, as we shall see.

But can the question be avoided? Inserting considerations of gender into discussions of poetry is, quite simply, what we do today. This is, of course, because of the woman's movement of the last 30 years, whose main concern has been to change the society we live in now, but it has also – inevitably – affected the way we look at the past. Which includes, of course, the way we think about literature.

The wider the range of what readers of poetry are sensitive to, the more the poem is enriched: so consciousness of gender should count as a gain in our reading. But all gains have a price. Settling down to read Donne's 16th Elegy, 'On his Mistress', the sensitive reader will be stirred by the magnificent sense of urgency in its opening lines:

By our first strange and fatal interview,
By all desires which thereof did ensue,
By our long starving hopes, by that remorse
Which my words masculine persuasive force
Begot in thee, and by the memory
Of hurts, which spies and rivals threatened me,
I calmly beg . . .

He is begging her not to disguise herself as a page and follow him on his dangerous journey: a situation that could come from an Elizabethan play, as could the dramatic quality of the writing. Staying home and distressed by his dangers, she may dream and frighten her nurse

> With midnight startings, crying out, oh, oh,
> Nurse, O my love is slain, I saw him go
> O'er the white Alps alone, I saw him, I,
> Assailed, fight, taken, stabb'd, bleed, fall, and die.

It is a vivid and wonderful poem, but few readers today, however much they may feel the energy of the lines, will fail to be pulled up by the fourth line: 'By my words masculine persuasive force'. Boasting of his linguistic vigour, he compares it to sexual vigour: look how well I write, it proves my virility. She stays home, while he is going to plunge into the kind of adventures only men can cope with, proving their virility by the masculinity of the syntax which announces their death. A true poet is a real man. Donne, to today's reader, looks like a male chauvinist.

But leaping a century ahead, we can put next to this one of the most famous condemnations of the 'metaphysical' poets: Dryden's complaint that Donne 'perplexes the mind of the fair sex with nice speculations of philosophy, when he should engage their hearts, and entertain them with the softnesses of love.' The sexism of this is sharp and obvious: metaphysics is not for women, they should be wooed with melody, sentiment and flattery. Dryden is not exactly praising the 'nice speculations': I'm not at all sure he would consider them welcome in an all-male gathering. But you do not need to show much enthusiasm for an intellectual activity in order to find it useful as a way of reminding women of their limitations: philosophy, it seems, has at least the merit of being one of the things women can't do.

Set against this, Donne can easily become a feminist hero. By blinding his women with supersubtle theology ('As an angel, face and wings Of air, not pure as it, yet pure, doth wear') he is making it clear that they are not his intellectual inferiors. His mistress will appreciate his words' masculine persuasive force, she dreams of death in language as vigorous as his. Blandishments and convention are all very well for Dryden's conventional women: real women are like real men, they enjoy sex, power and dramatic situations.

Donne the bully, Dryden the humane? Donne paying women the compliment of treating them as equals, Dryden keeping them in their place? How do we choose? That is an example of how feminist criticism could influence the way we read particular poems, even particular details. As well as this, it can change our view of which poems to read, that is, of the canon. Looking at the great tradition of English poetry, the feminist notices that it consists almost entirely of poems by men. Once this fact has thrust itself on our attention, how do we react? I suggest that there are four possible reactions, which I shall call conservative, individual recuperation, alternative canon and cultural recuperation.

The conservative claims that women's poems are justly excluded from the canon because they are not good enough. One T.H. Lister wrote in the *Edinburgh Review* in the mid 19th century: 'Experience does not authorize us to regard it as probable that the world will be favoured with any poetry of very exalted merit from persons in humble life and of defective education.' Lister was primarily concerned with peasant poets and working men writing memoirs, but his gesture of exclusion based on class could equally be based on gender: indeed most women would have qualified for the heading 'defective education'. It is unfashionable to be conservative on these matters, so I must begin by saying that this position is not necessarily stupid or thoughtless. It may spring from a passionate love of favourite poems (Gray's *Elegy*, perhaps, or Keats's Odes), and a conviction that to claim equal merit for other poems on what will seem to the conservative to be political rather than literary grounds is to cheapen poetry. The conservative may even deny that there are very many poems by women, pointing out that in patriarchal society writing poetry, like most things of importance, was done mainly by men; but this position is less certain than it looks: since the evidence we find depends on where we look, even on whether we look, it is not surprising that far more women's poetry, both published and unpublished, has been unearthed than a previous generation thought possible – most of it published, since it has never been true that publishers were unwilling to take on female authors.

It would seem a natural assumption that this conservative position is more likely to be held by men than by women, but the experience of teaching a course on women's poetry to an adult class consisting of 22 women and one man caused me to revise my view on this. Confronted by the poems of Katherine Philips, the matchless Orinda, they had no hesitation in taking them as evidence that plenty of women's poetry deserves to be forgotten; of Felicia Hemans they were even more contemptuous. 'Evening Prayer at a Girl's School', declared one member of my class, 'made me want to throw up'. I was even on one occasion accused of deliberately offering them bad poems in order to put women down.

3

That is the conservative position, and I here add that it need not imply conservatism on gender politics. The lack of good poems by women could, no doubt, be taken as evidence that women cannot write good poems, but it can equally be evidence of women's oppression, of their exclusion from respect and education. This is, for instance, the position of Germaine Greer, whom no-one, I take it, could accuse of conservatism on gender politics: 'The dilemma of the student of poetry who is also passionately interested in women is that she has to find value in a mass of work that she knows to be inferior . . . . The problem that confronts the student of women's creativity is not that there is no poetry by women, but that there is so much bad poetry by women.'

Second, there is individual recuperation: the admission that there are very good poems by women which patriarchal prejudice has sometimes prevented the Establishment from admiring, or even noticing. In one sense this too is a conservative position, since making claims for neglected works has always been a favourite pastime of literary criticism: each critic likes to feel that he has done his bit for a neglected author or two. This will only have radical implications if the recuperating includes the claim that the very criteria used to establish the orthodox canon need to be interrogated, that patriarchal prejudice has not simply involved ignoring women's poems, but has judged them by the wrong standards: that gives us the third position, the claim for an alternative canon.

Once we make that claim, there is no doubt of the subversive implications. Is there something inherently patriarchal about what we have traditionally expected of poems? A female poet once remarked to me that the reason another (and more successful) female poet had been so widely praised by the critics was that 'she writes like a man'. Just as Wordsworth, seeking to overthrow an Augustan standard that elevated the wrong sort of poetry to canonical status, asserted that an original poet needs to create the taste by which he is judged, so this poet wanted to create a new and more feminist taste. A new taste? The implications of this for literature will be (according to one's position) alarming or exhilarating.

This call for an alternative canon, judged by different criteria, is faced with two important and fascinating questions. First, what will it say about the female writers already accepted into the traditional canon (Madame de la Fayette, Jane Austen, Charlotte Brontë, George Eliot, Collette, in fiction; Elizabeth Browning, Christina Rossetti, Emily Dickinson, among others, in poetry)? Do they all 'write like men'? Do they differ from other, neglected female authors in the same way that Milton, Wordsworth or Tennyson differ from neglected male poets? Does their acceptance by patriarchal criticism represent a kind of betrayal of their status as women? And what did *they* think about the idea of an alternative canon? For Elizabeth Browning the idea was certainly objectionable. 'The divineness of poetry,' she wrote, 'is far more to me than either pride of sex or personal pride . . . And though I in turn suffer for this myself – though I too may be turned out of "Arcadia", and told that I am not a poet, still, I should be content, I hope, that the divineness of poetry be proved in my humanness, rather than lowered to my uses.'

And second, and more important: since an alternative canon implies alternative criteria, what are the patriarchal criteria for judging poetry, and what would the alternative, feminist criteria be? Is it a question of aesthetic qualities (simplicity rather than complexity, spontaneity rather than polish, directness rather than irony)? Or of subject matter? Reading the poetry of early 18th century women, and failing to discover any specifically feminine way of using language, I did realise that they had discovered a new subject for poetry: the experience of being trapped in marriage. This extension of the subject matter of poetry will engage us in Chapter 2.

The call for an alternative canon begins to overlap with what I propose as the fourth position, cultural recuperation. This is the claim that we should study poems by women simply because they are there, because they represent the achievement of a group. Do not ask how good they are, since this could distract us from the desirability of paying attention to them.

Indeed, cultural recuperation, as I am calling it, though often – and understandably – espoused by radicals, has in principle nothing radical about it. Interrogating the idea of permanent value in literature, seeing such claims to intrinsic and unchanging excellence as themselves historically determined, and even (in Foucauldian terms) as a strategy to enforce the claims of privileged groups to cultural power, has now become central to literary studies, and this question will necessarily engage us in the ensuing discussions. To study the past simply because it is there, not because it speaks to our condition, may seem radical and even subversive to the traditional literary humanist, but it is, after all, what historians have always done. The drive to cultural recuperation can be seen as a natural consequence of any historical interest. The fact that a text or an action from the past seems incomprehensible or tends to be misunderstood – the fact that it does *not* speak to our condition – often seems to the historian the strongest reason for studying it.

That outline is an attempt to map, schematically – as befits an introduction – the various positions from which one can approach the study of women's poetry. I hope the reader will not be too dismayed if I now say that this book has elements of all four. Welcoming enthusiastically the questions that feminist criticism invites us to ask, it insists on treating these as questions, with no built-in answers.

A word on the method, and the limitations, of this book. First, discussing poetry means discussing poems. The title announces that it is about reading, not forming theories about, women's poetry. If we form theories, they should spring from our reading of actual poems. There is more quotation than is usual in books about poetry, and although I cannot, alas, quote in full every poem I discuss, I have done my best to quote what is essential to the discussion. Second, comparison: we are now surrounded with anthologies of women's poetry, and books on women's writing and on the female tradition; and for the most part these juxtapose writings by women with writings by women. How else could they carry out their programme? But for everything there is a price; and the price in this case is avoiding the question of how, if at all, does women's poetry differ from men's? I therefore make frequent comparisons between poems by women and poems by men, not to assert the superiority of either, but to ask how (and whether) they differ. Third, the choice of poets: not wanting to offer a brief sentence or two on large numbers of poets, I have selected those I believe to be the best and most interesting, at the expense of leaving out others: hence Anne Finch, not Mary Leapor; Charlotte Mew, not Alice Meynell; Marianne Moore, not Edith Sitwell. The most difficult decision on who to omit concerned Felicia Hemans and Letitia Elizabeth Landon, the two most successful female poets of their time or any time, and this is briefly discussed at the beginning of the chapter on the nineteenth century. And not wanting either to gallop hastily over our own time, when there has been so much fine poetry by women, I have ended the book in the mid 20th century; dates are arbitrary, so I chose an arbitrary end point, and have included no poet younger than Sylvia Plath. Fourth, scholarly apparatus: although I hope this book will interest scholars and academics, it is in the first instance written for readers of poetry, and I did not want to alienate these by excessive scholarly annotation; so I have avoided footnotes. Those who wish to read further, or know where a poem can be found, will, I hope, find the necessary information in the note appended to most of the sections, and I have kept these brief. And there is one other omission, which needs rather more discussion.

Those engaged with recent feminist theory (post-structuralist, gyno-criticism, écriture feminine and related theories) will have noticed its absence from this introduction. I will put the reason for this at its bluntest: I have little sympathy with such theoretical movements, which often seem to be confused attempts to mingle the obvious with the dogmati-cally programmatic. Simply to say this is a dismissive gesture that to the theoretician will seem old-fashioned, and to the feminist theoretician will seem typical of patriarchy; but to explain and justify it at length would of course turn this book into the kind of theorising it wishes to avoid. The dilemma seems inescapable.

I will therefore look briefly now at the claim that *all* serious discus-sion of women's poetry should concern itself with feminist theory. The theoreticians should be allowed to speak for themselves, so I have chosen a single statement, Anita Pacheco's introduction to the collection of essays on *Early Women Writers* (1998).

Pacheco claims that the canon, 'far from springing spontaneously into existence is a cultural construct which has tended to reproduce and rein-force the marginalisation of women and other social groups'; that 'a woman's experience of oppression will somehow be inscribed in her writing'; that gynocriticism, or the study of women's writing without theorising its production (a category to which this book no doubt belongs) suffers from the limitation that it implicitly claims that a work of literature 'is a mirror on the author's life, giving the reader unmedi-ated access to the world in which she lived and wrote. In this . . . gynocriticism concurs with humanist ideology in seeing language as expressive of an external knowable reality and the author as the sole origin of textual meaning.' Structuralism and post-structuralism, on the other hand, premise 'that language and culture precede and shape the human subject and her experiences, and not the other way round'.

'Humanism' has become one of the commonest terms of reproach in radical literary theory; crudely, it is used to denote the view that the individual writer is autonomous rather than the product of social forces. Such thinkers as Foucault and Althusser are anti-humanist because they claim that 'ideology pervades our perception of reality, that it is located in material practices with material effects' – a claim that is 'clearly incompatible with humanist views of human nature: far from possess-ing a transhistorical essence, human beings are produced within a historically specific ideological formation which pre-exists and therefore shapes their experience.'

Such, briefly but mainly in her own words, is the general position that Pacheco sees as underlying the theoretically informed criticism she wishes to represent; my response is that in attacking the essentialising tendency of the humanist, her position does quite as much essentialising: she is free with adjectives (*unmediated* access, *sole* origin) that ascribe to the 'humanist' a rigid and dogmatic certainty. No doubt the humanism of which she is so critical did often in the past have a religious dimension, appealing to what is eternal and unchanging, but there is no reason why a modern humanism should not be as complex and subtle as any other theory. Looking back at earlier literature I find that some poems (by Shakespeare, Keats or Dickinson), though no doubt they were in part influenced by the 'historically specific ideological formation' which helped to shape them, speak to us more powerfully than other more pedestrian, more merely derivative poems. If it is 'humanist' to be moved by them, and to seek to retain that experience when we proceed to discuss and contextualise them, then every lover of poetry is a humanist.

The belief that language is 'expressive of an external knowable reality' is often attacked by post-structuralism. Is language, we may ask, a window, as the naïve often assume, or a prison-house, as the post-structuralist likes to assert? I have no doubt that it is both. I will take as a (necessarily brief) example the astronomical arguments in the 16th century about heliocentric versus geocentric theories. These were, we now realise, laden with social and even gender assumptions, but they were about external reality as well, and they have now been solved. We now know that the earth travels round the sun. Perhaps there are political and gender assumptions lurking in that sentence, though I cannot detect them. But the sentence is also true, and I doubt if there are many post-structuralist geocentrists today.

What of the traditional belief that language gives us 'unmediated access' to the world in which a poet lived and wrote? The delight of reading a poem that moves us does appear to give us immediate access to another consciousness, and I would be suspicious of any critic who never felt that; but when we pause and reflect then we all become aware that this access is mediated by language: it needs no post-structuralist come from Yale to tell us that. He will of course tell us that this access is mediated by conventions and assumptions that we may not share, and also, as Foucault will tell us, by the presence of power. I believe that discussing poetry should explore these mediations without losing sight of the immediacy of our reading experience.

I will mention one other claim, made by Selden and Smith in their General Editors' Preface to Pacheco's book. Very conscious of literature as an object of academic study, they discuss the place of literary theory in 'the agenda of literary studies'. 'We can no longer pretend that we all tacitly accept the same practices in literary studies. A *laissez-faire* attitude is no longer tenable. Literature departments need to go beyond the mere toleration of theoretical differences . . . .they need actually to "stage openly" the differences in theoretical approach. ' Well, theoretical positions are always worth studying, and the more philosophically minded will enjoy the arguments. The experience of reading and responding, however, precedes (or should precede) attempts to 'theorise' it. 'Staging openly' the conflict between pre- and post-Copernican explanations of the earth's movement can be fascinating, but we need not expect modern astronomers to take a great interest in it, if they feel they have better things to do.

All experiences can be placed in a theoretical context, but that does not abolish the experience. The diner who enjoys his meal might read books on chemistry in cooking, or discussions of the economic functions of restaurants in our society; the lover might read Foucault on sexuality; even the football fan might read books on the place of football in the modern industrialised economy: none of this abolishes the experience of enjoying one's meal, or of sexual intercourse, or watching Ronaldo play. When I was teaching at an American university I discussed with a colleague his theoretically sophisticated work on Wordsworth. At one point I remarked that what he was doing was very interesting to the academic student of Wordsworth, but asked what he thought it said to the non-academic reader – and lover – of Wordsworth's poetry. His reply was honest and almost wistful: that he had never met a reader of Wordsworth who was not either an academic or a student. My book is written in the belief that there are lovers of poetry as well as academic students of literature, and that the literary academic should be a poetry lover as well. That discussions of poetry start with discussions of poems.

Note on Reading   The best anthology of women's writing (containing prose as well as poetry, and coming right up to the present time) is probably *The Norton Anthology of Literature by Women*, edited by Sandra M. Gilbert and Susan Gubar (Yale, 1979). It is very fully annotated, often usefully, perhaps excessively (one might wonder what those students who need to be told that Adam and Eve were the first man and first woman according to the Bible will make of some of the poems.) Also valuable (and shorter) is *Everywoman's Poetry: Elizabethan to Victorian,* ed R.E. Pritchard (Fyfield Books, Manchester, 1990).

Interest in women's writing has led to a number of period anthologies of women's poetry, some of them very full:

Early Modern Women Poets, 1520–1700, edited by Jane Stevenson & Peter Davidson (Oxford, 2001).

Eighteenth Century Women Poets, edited by Roger Lonsdale (Oxford, 1989).

Women Romantic Poets, 1785–1832, ed. Jennifer Breen (Dent: Everyman, 1992).

Romantic Woman Poets, 1770–1838, ed. Andrew Ashfield (Manchester University Press, 1995).

British Women Poets of the Romantic Era ed. Paula R. Feldman (Johns Hopkins Univerity Press, 1997).

Romantic Women Poets: An Anthology ed. Duncan Wu (Blackwell, 1997).

Nineteenth Century Women Poets: an Oxford Anthology, ed. Isobel Armstrong and others (Oxford, 1996)

Victorian Women Poets: An Anthology, ed. Angela Leighton and Margaret Reynolds (Blackwell, 1991).

Though there are a good many books about women's writing, some of them very influential, and a good number on specific periods of women's poetry (some of these are recommended in later notes), there are surprisingly few general histories or discussions of women's poetry; perhaps the best – eccentric but fitfully brilliant – is Germaine Greer, *Slip-shod Sibyls: Recognition, Rejection and the Woman Poet* (Viking, 1995). Two very influential books on women's writing (dealing with prose more than poetry) are Elaine Showalter: *A Literature of their Own* (Virago 1977) and Ellen Moers: *Literary Women* (The Women's Press, 1978). Perhaps the most influential of all, though dealing only with the nineteenth century, is Gilbert and Gubar: *The Madwoman in the Attic* (Yale, 1979), whose position can be indicated by a sentence from their first chapter: 'If the pen is a metaphorical penis, with what organ can females generate texts?'

There are however some very stimulating introductions to anthologies of women's poetry: Cora Kaplan's to *Salt and Bitter and Good* (Paddington Press, 1975); Fleur Adcock's to *The Faber Book of 20th Century Women's Poetry* (Faber, 1987); and Emma Donoghue's to *What Sappho Would Have Said* (Hamish Hamilton, 1997).

1

The Beginnings

The first Englishwoman to achieve fame as a poet was Katherine Philips, 'the matchless Orinda'. Her poems appeared in an unauthorised edition in 1664, and were reissued in 1667, five years after her death from smallpox at the age of 33, introduced by a large apparatus of dedicatory poems, all of which say the same thing:

> We allow'd you beauty, and we did submit
>   To all the tyrannies of it.
> Ah cruel Sex! will you dispose us too in Wit?
>   Orinda does in that too reign,
> Does man behind her in proud triumph draw,
> And cancel great Apollo's Salic Law . . . .
>
>   Thou glory of our sex, envy of men,
> Who are both pleas'd and vex'd with thy bright pen:
> Its lustre doth entice their eyes to gaze,
> But men's sore eyes cannot endure its rays;
> It dazzles and surprises so with light,
> To find a noon where they expected night . . .

Insisting on the unusualness of such accomplished writing coming from a woman is no doubt flattering to her as an individual, but still assumes that writing poetry, like most talents, belongs normally to men. The vocabulary of these compliments – 'cruel', 'tyrannies', and the military images that are developed at length – is that of love poetry, which congratulates a woman on her conquest over men's hearts, bestowing on her a metaphorical power in a world in which she has no real power. Her writing talent is thus assimilated to sexual attraction, instead of granting to her a power other than sexual.

Congratulatory verses are always unlikely to break new ground imaginatively, and we need not be hard on the well-intentioned men (and women!) who wrote these introductory poems, using the terminology that came most readily to hand, and so did nothing to transcend conventional limitations. But what of Philips' own poems? Do they, more than those who paid her compliments, offer an imaginative breakthrough?

The volume contains conventional prayers in verse, political poems, including a lament about the death of Charles I (her politics were royalist, though her husband was a Puritan and a member of Barebones' Parliament), praises of country life, and, most frequent and most impressive, celebrations of friendship addressed to real women under such poetical names as Lucasia and Rosania. Some of these caught the eye of Keats, who contrasted Philips with 'a set of Devils' who have 'vexed and teased our England within the last 30 years' – women who 'set themselves up for towers of Babel in languages, Sapphos in poetry – Euclids in geometry and everything in nothing.'. Here we have the opposite both to the complimentary verses and to much modern feminism: Keats has enjoyed her poems, but does not use her to question the general prejudice against women's poetry.

Her poems of Platonic friendship celebrate a union of souls:

> Our chang'd and mingled souls are grown
>   To such acquaintance now,
> That if each would resume their own,
>   Alas! we know not how.
> We have each other so engrost
>   That each is in the union lost   TO MRS M.A. AT PARTING

> I did not live until this time
>   Crown'd my felicity,
> When I could say without a crime,
>   I am not thine, but Thee.

> This carcass breath'd, and walkt, and slept,
>   So that the World believ'd
> There was a soul the motions kept;
>   But they were all deceiv'd.   TO MY EXCELLENT LUCASIA,
>   ON OUR FRIENDSHIP

Philips' model was William Cartwright, who was twenty years her senior, and who also died in his early thirties. Cartwright wrote anti-Platonist poems, which (at least to a coarse-minded reader) seem inevitably livelier than the uplifting insistence on union of souls:

Tell me no more of Minds embracing Minds,
  And hearts exchanged for hearts . . .

Come, I will undeceive thee, they that tread
  These vain Aeriall waies . . .
For searching thus to be for ever Rich,
  They only find a medicine for the Itch.

The fact that Philips was a disciple of Cartwright can hardly seem of much importance today, when he is as forgotten as she is. What she took from him was clearly stylistic and technical, ignoring his rather jocular anti-Platonism, and he is such a representative figure that she could as easily have taken it from those who lie behind him. Speaking of herself as a 'carcass' before Lucasia breathed a soul into her could come from Donne; the celebration of their union by declaring 'We have each other so engrost That each is in the union lost' could come from Sidney, or Donne, or the Shakespeare of 'The Phoenix and the Turtle'. As much wit as Donne or Marvell puts into one stanza, however, will usually last Philips for a whole poem: an urbane, polished, mildly witty poem, touched with philosophy.

It would certainly be an oversimplification to describe the poems of the down-to-earth Cartwright as masculine and those of the Platonist Philips as feminine, since there is plenty of Renaissance poetry by men that celebrates a union of souls in Neoplatonist terms, either a union between friends of the same sex, or a union between men and women that can do without sex. What we can ask is how the tradition of friendship as a union of souls changes when the friendship is between women, not men.

There is a convenient way of answering this. In his *Discourse of the Nature and Offices of Friendship* (1657) Jeremy Taylor sets forth the ideal of 'a dear and perfect friendship', stating it (as befits a clergyman) in more explicitly Christian terms than was customary, but using many of the commonplaces of the time. Friendship between men can be seen as a union of souls, since it can be described without mention of the body; friendship between man and woman lacks this advantage, and is therefore complicated by questions of prudence: it must be conducted 'so that he shall rather lose much of his own comfort than she anything of her honour'. But what of friendship between two women?

As Taylor introduces each section of his discussion he writes 'brother or sister', 'man or woman', and then continues using masculine pronouns only: this was of course normal, and remained so until the later 20th century. Taylor was a friend of Philips, and wrote the essay for her, and it therefore includes a section which asks explicitly whether women too can be partners in a noble friendship. His answer draws distinctions which seem to derive more from preconceptions about gender than from much actual observation ('a man is the best friend in trouble, but a woman may be equal to him in the days of joy'), and concludes that since 'few persons in the world have all these excellencies by which friendship can be useful and illustrious, we may as well allow women as men to be friends' (in fairness to Taylor, we need to exclude the modern colloquial use of 'may as well', with its suggestion of grudging concession). Taylor assumes that friendship is a masculine quality, but is willing to grant that it can be found in women – that is as much, perhaps, as can be expected.

This is the context in which Philips' poems of female friendship should be placed: the extension of a masculine tradition to include women, rather than the assertion of a different tradition. But poems, though read in context, are able to modify the context they use, so we can ask if those of Philips fit obediently into expectations. Here is 'Friendship in Emblem, or the Seal: to my dearest Lucasia':

> The Compasses that stand above,
> Express this great immortal Love;
> For friends, like them, can prove this true,
> They are, and yet they are not, two.
>
> And in their posture is expressed
> Friendship's exalted interest:
> Each follows where the other leans,
> And what each does, this other means.
>
> And as when one foot does stand fast,
> And th'other circles seeks to cast,
> The steady part does regulate
> And makes the wand'rer's motion straight:
>
> So friends are only two in this,
> T'reclaim each other when they miss:
> For whosoe'er will grossly fall,
> Can never be a friend at all.
>
> And as that useful instrument
> For even lines was ever meant;

> So Friendship from good Angels springs,
> To teach the world heroic things.

This image derives, of course, from Donne's famous comparison between lovers parted and a pair of compasses. Has she altered the significance of the image, in shifting it from heterosexual love to female friendship? This is a natural question for us today, and it is very difficult to answer. 'A quick and simple feminist reading', claims Elaine Hobby of Donne's poem, 'would point out how the compasses actually celebrate woman's immobility and fixity in "the centre", and man's freedom to move and still be loved.' This would indeed be a simple, even a simplistic, feminist reading, since it could equally be claimed that they celebrate the control which the fixed foot exerts over the moving one. In Philips this is almost explicit: the fixed foot 'regulates' the other. Donne's poem celebrates a love which does not depend on 'sense', but is 'inter-assuréd of the mind' and can therefore survive bodily parting, so there seems no reason why it should not apply to same-sex friendship; just as it would not be difficult to imagine Philips' poem of friendship as a love-poem.

If we compare Philips' poem with the most famous poem of friendship in the English 17th century, Jonson's Ode 'To the Immortal Memory and Friendship of that Noble Pair, Sir Lucius Cary, and Sir H Morison', we find them both using a generalised celebration of union ('Till either grew a portion of the other', says one: 'Each stiled by his end The Coppie of his friend' says the other); but Jonson also gives us much more information about the lives of the two friends: Philips' friendship with Lucasia, lacking specifics, seems indistinguishable from that with Rosalia. At least one difference between the two poets can, perhaps, be related to gender: Jonson offers a garland, clearly meant to be worn in public, and he concludes by claiming that Cary and Morison were an example to others, who 'might read and find / Friendship indeed was written, not in words; And with the heart, not pen.' Female friendship, as described by Philiips, is much more private: the two friends live for each other, but we are not told that they are an example to the world. Is this just a difference between two poems, or is it a reminder that female experience is necessarily more private than male? If so, it would of course resemble sexual love: "Twere profanation of our joys / To tell the laity our love', as Donne famously wrote. Men live with men in the public world: men live with women as women live with women, in a private world.

This may be as true as such generalisations ever are: but Orinda also praises female friendship in ways that seem to contrast it with marriage:

Nobler than Kindred or than Marriage-band,
   Because more free. Wedlock-felicity
Itself doth only by this Union stand,
   And turns to Friendship or to Misery.
Force or Design Matches to pass may bring,
  But Friendship doth from Love and Honour spring.

This is a more interesting (and more radical) assertion than may at first appear. It contrasts friendship not simply with marriage, but specifically with 'wedlock-felicity', which must surely mean – or at least include – sexual consummation. The view of marriage here offered is strikingly similar to Mary Wollstonecraft's feminist assertion a century and a half later: 'Love, from its very nature, must be transitory . . . The most holy band of society is friendship.' For Wollstonecraft, once the intensity of passion is over, friendship not love (that 'common passion, in which chance and sensation take place of choice and reason') is the proper basis of marriage. For Philips, too, the joys of the honeymoon ('wedlock felic-ity') do not last: marriage must then turn into friendship or into misery. The analogy between female friendship and successful marriage, asserted as a feminist discovery by Wollstonecraft out of her own painful experi-ence of sexual betrayal, has been anticipated by Philips (whose marriage to a much older man was, as far as we know, a happy one).

    There is of course one other logical possibility, that of friendship between a man and a woman who have never had a sexual relationship; and at least one 17th century poem asserts the possibility of this: 'To Phylocles, inviting him to Friendship', by Ephelia (it is not known who either of these is, but Phylocles is clearly male and Ephelia female).

    Best of thy sex! If Sacred Friendship can
    Dwell in the Bosom of inconstant Man . . .
    We will forget the Difference of Sex,
    Nor shall the World's rude Censure us Perplex:
    Think me all Man: my soul is Masculine,
    And Capable of as great Things as Thine.

A poem that protests too much defeats its own purpose. Can friendship between man and woman ignore sex? A poem that believes it can needs itself to ignore sex, which this poem signally fails to do. Perhaps such a poem might be possible today, in a world where men and women can be colleagues or intellectual equals, but Ephelia's insistences make it all too clear that her poem does not belong in such a world.

Among these virtuous wives and chaste friends, one woman stands out as a vivid and shocking contrast. Aphra Behn's adventurous and unorthodox life included a youth spent in Surinam, and a spell as a government spy among the Dutch. When alive, she may well have deserved her reputation as a loose woman; posthumously, she certainly deserves the more important distinction of being the first Englishwoman to earn her living by her pen. She was a prolific and successful playwright, and the author of several prose fictions: compared with this, her poems, mostly from her plays, are marginal. They are also highly erotic, and if not quite as openly indecent as the most shocking poems of her friend the Earl of Rochester, they were enough to add to Behn's reputation as a loose woman. A song from her play *The Dutch Lover* is simply a woman's account of being seduced:

> A many kisses did he give
> And I returned the same,
> Which made me willing to receive
> That which I dare not name.

The Disappointment, a rather longer poem, imitated from the French, is simply an account of a man being overcome by impotence. Also from the French – rather freely, and more indecent than the original – is her longest poem, *A Voyage to the Isle of Love.* Her oddest, and perhaps her most indecent, poem, is *To the Fair Clarinda, Who Made Love to Me, Imagined More than Woman,* which merits more discussion.

> Fair lovely maid, or if that title be
> Too weak, too feminine, for nobler thee,
> Permit a name that more approaches truth:
> And let me call thee lovely charming youth.
> This last will justify my soft complaint,
> While that may serve to lessen my constraint;
> And without blushes I the youth pursue,
> When so much beauteous woman is in view.

This teasing poem is obviously about sexual transgression, and obviously invites us to be shocked; but what exactly is it saying? We can begin with a lexical point, that before the mid 20th century to 'make love', which today usually means to have sexual intercourse, more often referred to what was said, not what was done, and meant to court or to woo: the title therefore need not (but perhaps could) refer to lesbianism. When we are being teased – as we clearly are here – we need to know what we can be sure of: titles do not normally lie, so I take it that it is about two women being in bed together. The modern reader, used to a culture in which unmarried girls, if not indulging in sexual intercourse, sleep alone, needs to begin with a reminder that sleeping alone was much rarer in earlier centuries, so for Clarinda to be the speaker's bedfellow is not unusual. But no amount of historicizing can deny that the title is meant to shock, or that some pretending is going on:

> Against thy charms we struggle but in vain;
> With thy deluding form thou givest us pain,
> While the bright nymph betrays us to the swain.
> In pity to our sex thou sure wert sent,
> That we might love, and yet be innocent.
> For sure no crime with thee we can commit,
> Or if we should – thy form excuses it.
> For who that gathers fairest flowers believes
> A snake lies hid beneath the fragrant leaves.

The poem grows even stranger as it proceeds: the logic of what it has so far said suggests that the male form excuses the lesbian attraction, but that last couplet has so obvious a sexual suggestion (the snake beneath the leaves being a familiar image for the male seen sexually) that the poem seems to have changed sides: now the male principle is the threat, and the female body is the innocent flower.

The poem ends by joining together the two ways of seeing Clorinda:

> Thou beauteous wonder of a different kind,
> Soft Cloris with the dear Alexis joined;
> Whene'er the manly part of thee would plead
> Thou tempts us with the image of the maid,
> While we the noblest passions do extend
> The love to Hermes, Aphrodite the friend.

The wordplay on which the poem ends is a reminder that the word *hermaphrodite* is formed by joining together the names of Hermes and Aphrodite, so that to imagining Clorinda as a man is something that has already been done by the language. And who, in the poem, does the imagining? The poet, obviously, but when? Did she imagine Clorinda as a man when actually in bed with her, so as to enjoy the Lesbian experience while pretending that it was heterosexual? Or does she do the imagining by writing the poem, casting a retrospective legitimacy over a transgression already committed? And are we right – was the poem right? – to see it as legitimising? Is Lesbianism so outrageous that it makes ordinary sexual misbehaviour seem proper?

A poem about changing shape and about guilt disguised as innocence could operate with a consistent logic or a deliberate defying of consistency, and discussions of such a poem may often disagree (more often than they admit) which is the more powerful poetically. This poem has, unsurprisingly, attracted critics interested in sexual dissidence, and they do not always agree on which is (or on which the poem sees as) the more subversive, coupling with a man or with another woman.

That Aphra Behn was the most indecent female poet of her time (and of many subsequent times) can hardly be doubted. Does that makes her the best – or the worst – or not necessarily either?

Back now to Philips, and to two other poems that should catch the eye of the modern reader. Her son Hector died in infancy:, and she wrote a couple of epitaphs on him.

> Twice forty months of wedlock did I stay
> Then had my vows crowned with a lovely boy.
> And yet in forty days he dropt away;
> O swift vicissitude of human joy!
>
> I did but see him, and he disappeared,
> I did but pluck the rosebud and it fell;
> A sorrow unforeseen and scarcely fear'd,
> For ill can mortals their affliction spell.

There is no wit here, not even the diluted wit of the friendship poems, and the effect depends on a quiet, direct dignity: in which the simplest lines are the most moving: 'I did but pluck the rosebud, and it fell'. Yet she ends:

> Receive these gasping numbers to thy grave,
> The last of thy unhappy mother's verse.

'Gasping numbers': does this mean that she is gasping – with grief – or is it an apology for the fact that the 'numbers' are gasping: that the metre limps? But the numbers do not gasp: the poem is metrically very accomplished.

As are the domestic poems of Anne Bradstreet, celebrating (a few years later) her love for her husband and expressing her grief at the death of grandchildren. Philips is the first English woman poet to achieve fame, and Bradstreet is well known as the first American – indeed, the first American poet of either sex. Yet her Americanism is not very important: the Puritan culture in which she lived was not yet very different on the two sides of the Atlantic, and she would probably have written very similar poems had she remained in the land of her birth. Indeed, her poems were published in England before they appeared in America: a volume called *The Tenth Muse lately Sprung up in America* appeared anonymously in London in 1650, without her name ('By a Gentlewoman in those parts'). As so often, we do not know how far she consented to the publication, and there is the usual disclaimer, telling us that the book was 'snatched' by friends and 'expos'd to public view', at which 'my blushing was not small'. Most of the volume consists of long philosophical poems in the manner of Du Bartas, whom she greatly admired, on the four Elements, the four Humours, the four Ages of man, and other 'quaternions' – a concept as ponderous as the name suggests. They are seldom read today, and her fame rests on the poems about her family, in which she appears as a loving and dutiful wife, a loving grandmother, and a competent writer of couplets:

> If ever two were one, then surely we.
> If ever man were loved by wife, then thee;
> If ever wife was happy in a man,
> Compare with me ye women if you can . . .
> 'ON MY DEAR AND LOVING HUSBAND'

> No sooner come, but gone, and fal'n asleep,
> Acquaintance short, yet parting caus'd us weep,
> Three flowers, two scarcely blown, the last i'th'bud,
> Cropt by th'Almightie's hand; yet is he good,
> With dreadful awe before him let's be mute,
> Such was his will, but why, let's not dispute.
> 'ON MY DEAR GRAND-CHILD SIMON BRADSTREET'

It is hardly surprising that these women wrote poems of grief about infant death: so many of them must have experienced it. Child death became one of the central themes of literature in the 19th century; in the 17th, when more children died, it was not an established topos, as it later became, and the laments are mainly by women. This is hardly surprising: the death of an infant is almost certain to mean more to the mother than to the father, both because the physical bond is so intense, and also because the event belongs to domestic, not to public life – that is, to the world which the women inhabited.

There is of course no direct correlation between grief and poetic talent: and what are arguably the finest poems on child death in the century are by Ben Jonson (on his son, on his daughter, and on a child actor). But it is difficult to read the poems of Philips and Bradstreet in a spirit of judicious evaluation, for they offer us a glimpse into the culture of women that it is not easy to obtain. They wrote their laments in simple and dignified verse; but we might feel that a different kind of value attaches to 'gasping numbers' – an absence of polish springing from women's lack of (freedom from?) rhetorical training.

> *Written by me at the death of my 4th sonne and 5th Child Perigrene Payler.*
> I thought my all was given before
>   but mercy ordered me one more:
> A Perigrene: my God me sent
>   him back again I do present
> as a love token; 'mongst my others,
>   One Daughter; and hir 4 deare Brothers;
> To my Lord Christ; my only bless;
>   Is, he is mine; and am his
> My Dearest Lord; hast thou fulfill'd thy will,
>   thy hand maid's pleas'd. Compleatly happy still.
>   MARY CAREY (PAYLER)

This poem was never published, and we owe the text to the researches of modern feminist scholars. Here the numbers are certainly gasping: the broken syntax and halting metre seem possessed by the helplessness of grief.

It is hard to speak with certainty about a text like this. In an age when spelling and punctuation had not yet been regularised, we cannot be sure whether the irregularities are normal, or whether they show the female subculture with its lack of formal education, or whether they are the halting voice of grief. Certainly we have a poem by Mary's husband (also unpublished) on the same subject, which is much more regular in both syntax and metre, and which urges 'free submission to God's holy Will': submissive to God's command and her husband's, as befits a 'handmaid', Mary in turn declares herself, without even a main verb, 'compleatly happy still'. She cannot submit without reminding herself of the other children she has lost; she cannot see her loss as a blessing without breaking the word in the middle (here I must admit that 'bless' is not unknown as a substantive in the 17th century, but it is certainly rare); she cannot think of the child's name (meaning 'pilgrim') without pausing to break the syntax and contemplate the word. Her clumsiness is deeply moving; or do we exaggerate the clumsiness because we are moved, and because we seem for a moment to be given a true glimpse of the largely hidden world of women?

At some time in the 1630s a woman called Mary Price (née Cromwell) gave birth to a daughter; and her sister Elizabeth sent her a poem of congratulation and New Year greeting. It begins by dwelling on the name Mary:

> O gracious meek blest mary, a mother mild I may thee call
> Religious, charitable, humble, a dove that hath no gall,
> From these perfections mayst thou never starte
> The worlds encumbrances taketh not thy heart.

It is a very pious poem, wishing the happy mother a life of grace leading to everlasting bliss. Here is the conclusion:

> Now happie Mary, invessed
> In those white robes which best thee sute
> Emblems of purity a choice fruite
> This is thy newyearsgifte or Elizabeths salute.

There are, we now know, hundreds of verses like this by 17th century women: they have been rescued from oblivion by the devoted labours of modern scholars: in this case, by Jane Stevenson and Peter Davidson. Why?

There are two different answers to this. The historian's answer values every bit of writing from the past, since it will form an item, however tiny, in the picture we build of what it was like to be a woman, a Protestant, a mother, a sister, in 17th century England. The more material we have, the fuller our picture of the age, and nothing brings the life of women more vividly and painfully before us than the poems they wrote about their children (or, in the case of Elizabeth Cromwell, nieces). They offer us a shiver of authenticity.

In contrast to this there is what would traditionally have been called the literary answer. Among the millions of words written in 17th century England, some use language to relate experience with unusual power and aptness, standing out from the thousands of pages whose life is only as evidence. This contrast is old and familiar, though it has fallen into neglect of late: recent critics, and especially the new historicists, are not as confident about it as we once were. It has become common practice in literary studies not to rescue a poem from but to return it to its age, exploring not the differences but the similarities between the language of poems and that of sermons, legal documents and personal letters. We owe much to this insight, but we also pay a price, and rescuing the forgotten poems of 17th century women raises the issue in a sharp and even painful way.

> *A Grace for a Child*
> Here a little child I stand,
> Heaving up my either hand;
> Cold as paddocks though they be,
> Here I lift them up to Thee,
> For a Benison to fall
> On our meat, and on us all.

This is a gem of a poem. The child who speaks feels how cold his hands are, remembers that he once touched a frog and how cold it was, and perhaps gives a little shiver of remembering but does not let it stop his prayer; as he puts his hands together to pray, he feels the slight effort of raising them and registers it as sensation: hence 'heaving', and we feel its aptness even as, like the child, we do not let it distract us from the prayer. That there should be so much feeling, so much delicacy, so much sympathy, in six short lines, is a marvel. We call such marvels poetry.

This gem is by Robert Herrick, who never married, is not known to have had any children, and is writing not from his own painful experience, but because of what he saw, and sympathised with, the sight of a child praying. It has none of the painful authenticity of Mary Carey's poem on her son; her poem has none of the magic of Herrick's. Our reasons for valuing the one are different from those for valuing the other, but this need not mean dismissing either. Herrick's poem is, in an important sense, inauthentic, but to dismiss it for that reason is philistine; Mary Carey and Elizabeth Cromwell are irredeemably clumsy, but to dismiss their writing for that reason is callous.

Note *Poems by the most deservedly Admired Mrs Katherine Philips The Matchless Orinda* was published in 1667. I have used this edition and modernised its spelling. The remarks by Keats are from a letter to John Hamilton Reynolds, 21 September 1817. William Cartwright's 'No Platonic Love' is from his *Comedies, Tragi-Comedies, with other Poems* 1651. Jeremy Taylor's *Discourse of the Nature and Offices of Friendship, In a letter to the most ingenious excellent MKP* was published in 1657. The remark by Elaine Hobby is from her *Virtue of Necessity: English Women's writing 1649–1688* (Virago, 1988). Ben Jonson's Ode 'To the Immortal Memory of that Noble Pair, Sir Lucius Cary and Sir H. Morison' appeared in his *Works,* 1640, Mary Wollstonecraft's remark is from *A Vindication of the Rights of Women* (1792) chapter 2. The works of Aphra Behn are edited by Janet Todd, of which Vol. I (London, 1992) is devoted to her poems. *The Tenth Muse* (London 1650) was reissued posthumously with additional poems in Boston in 1678; I have taken the text from *Poems of Anne Bradstreet,* ed. Robert Hutchinson (New York, 1969). Poems on the death of children are discussed at length in my book *Angels and Absences* (Vanderbilt University Press, 1997).

Poems by 17th century women are reprinted in the two large collections, *Kissing the Rod* and *Early Modern Women Poets,* cited in the note to the Introduction.

2

Augustan & Romantic

The really outstanding women poets come in the 19th and 20th centuries, but there is no shortage of interesting and accomplished women in the 18th, often with a finger on the taste of the times – like, for instance, Anne Finch, countess of Winchilsea.

Anne Finch

Augustan civilisation constantly asserted its valuing of order, good sense and reason; Augustan poetry is dominated by the heroic couplet as no other period of English poetry, before or since, has been dominated by a single metrical pattern. It is not difficult to see the connexion: the regularity of the couplet, its ability to allow and control subtle variations of stress while relentlessly asserting the basic pattern, offers a clear analogy to the tyranny of reason, the relentless need to control the passions.

An Augustan poet who wished to escape the tyranny of the couplet, or of any other regular verse pattern, would write a Pindaric Ode: a fairly long poem in irregular rhymed verse, patterned, ostensibly, on the wild and irregular Odes of Pindar. Whether Pindar's Odes are really as irregular as they seem is a question for classical scholars: the 18th century saw them as irregular, and used the Ode as a licence to escape into freer form.

The commonest subject for Pindaric Odes was a passion, or, as we would probably say today, an emotion: William Collins wrote odes to Pity, to Fear, to Mercy, to Peace and even to the Passions; Thomas Gray's two Pindaric Odes, *The Bard* and *The Progress of Poetry,* have a narrative element, but are as irregular and as full of abstract nouns as Odes were supposed to be. Looking back, we might feel a little sceptical at the confidence with which emotions were classified and named: are there as many identifiable emotions as we have abstract nouns for them? Is not intense emotion by its very nature unclassifiable, a state resistant to the classifying spirit that devises abstract nouns? Does not our modern concept of the bipolar recognise the ease with which one uncontrollable emotional state can turn into its opposite? If then we ask whether the Augustans had a term that denoted not only emotional intensity but the instability of our classifying, the tendency of one emotion to turn into its opposite, the answer is that they did: spleen.

If ever subject and poetic form were made for each other, surely Spleen was made for the Pindaric Ode: yet I know of only one Pindaric Ode to Spleen. It is by Anne Finch, Countess of Winchilsea, and it begins with an admission that our terminology fails to pin down our experience:

> What art thou, Spleen, which ev'ry thing dost ape,
>   Thou Proteus to abused mankind;
>   Who never yet thy real cause could find,
> Or fix thee to remain in one continued shape?

Spleen varies as does the manic-depressive between 'a calm of stupid discontent' and 'a panic fear'. The second of its irregular stanzas blames the Fall: unfallen Adam could not be shocked by odours, but

> Now the jonquil o'ercomes the feeble brain;
> We faint beneath the aromatic pain

two magical lines that assert the vulnerability of the body, and establish Finch's poetic power.

The third stanza offers a startlingly frank picture of emotional conflict in marriage:

> In the imperious wife thou vapours art
>   Which from o'er-heated passions rise
>   In clouds to the attractive brain,
>   Until descending thence again,
> Through the o'er-cast and show'ring eyes,
>   Upon her husband's softened heart,
>   He the disputed point must yield,
> Something resign of the contested field;
> Till lordly man, born to imperial sway,
> Compounds for peace, to make that right away,
> And woman, armed with Spleen, does servilely obey.

'Vapours' – a manifestation of the always Protean spleen – was a fashionable term for female moodiness, here issuing in tears and conquering 'lordly man', forcing him to 'compound for peace' and to obey woman 'armed with Spleen':' the lines show us 'woman's weapons, water drops' (is Finch remembering *King Lear?*) overcoming 'lordly man' – one of the effects of spleen. No doubt the happily married and conventional Finch saw this as improper behaviour by the wife, but it is difficult to prevent the modern reader from taking 'lordly man, born to imperial sway' iron-ically, and nodding approval of at least one female victory.

In the fourth stanza the poem speaks about its own writing:

> O'er me alas! thou does too much prevail:
> I feel thy force, while I against thee rail;
> I feel my verse decay, and my cramped numbers fail.
> Through thy black jaundice I all objects see
> As dark and terrible as thee.

But failure, of course, is also success: the more the poet loses control of what she is writing, the more effectively she is expressing the power of spleen, which leads her to neglect her feminine tasks:

> Whilst in the Muses' paths I stray
> Whilst in their groves, and by their secret springs
> My hand delights to trace unusual things,
> And deviates from the known, and common way;
> Nor will in fading silks compose
> Faintly th'inimitable rose . . .

Another magical touch: the feminine tasks, like embroidery, which she really ought to busy herself with, now seem futile, but movingly futile, touched with natural evanescence. Spleen is both a distraction from normal duties and a revelation of the futility of human endeavour:

> Fill up an ill-drawn bird, or paint on glass
> The sovereign's blurred and undistinguished face,
> The threatening angel, and the speaking ass.

Painting biblical or patriotic scenes on glass is what spleen interferes with. She apologises; but she has been given a glimpse of the futility of her feminine life: her paintings on glass are not very good, and the sover-eign's face is so badly done that it cannot easily be recognised – or may we even speculate whether 'undistinguished ' here has what has become its commoner meaning, and she is telling us not that she's a rather bad painter, but that she doesn't think much of King William III. She probably didn't, and this meaning of 'undistinguished' dates from 1600, but I fear this reading is too mischievous.

The Pindaric Ode on spleen seems to me her most interesting poem, but it is laboured, as Pindaric odes so often are. The other extreme would be a short and pithy poem, like *Adam Posed:*

> Could our first father, at his toilsome plough,
> Thorns in his path, and labour on his brow
> Clothed only in a rude unpolished skin,
> Could he a vain fantastic nymph have seen,
> In all her airs, in all her antic graces,
> Her various fashions, and more various faces;
> How had it posed that skill, which late assigned
> Just appellations to each several kind,
> A right idea of the sight to frame;
> T' have guessed from what new element she came,
> T' have hit the wavering form, or given this thing a name.

Perhaps this poem took its origin from the middle-aged disapproval uttered by Finch's friends – or husband – reacting to the latest fashion – 'What would Adam have said if he'd seen *her?*' A rather thin subject for a poem? But at least a variant on the constantly recurring shepherds and shepherdesses of pastoral convention.

Furious Sappho: Pope and Lady Mary

Here are two passages about what it was like to be a woman in early 18th century fashionable society.

> Pleasures the sex, as children birds, pursue,
> Still out of reach, yet never out of view;
> Sure, if they catch, to spoil the toy at most,
> To covet flying, and regret when lost:
> At last, to follies youth could scarce defend,
> It grows their age's prudence to pretend;
> Ashamed to own they gave delight before,
> Reduced to feign it, when they give no more:
> As hags hold Sabbaths, less for joy than spite,
> So these their merry, miserable night;

Still round and round the ghosts of beauty glide,
And haunt the places where their honour died.

.   .   .

From whence is this unjust distinction grown?
Are we not formed with passions like your own?
Nature with equal fire our souls endued,
Our minds as haughty, and as warm our blood,
O're the wide world your pleasures you pursue,
The change is justified by something new;
But we must sigh in silence – and be true.
Our sex's weakness you expose and blame
(Of every prattling fop the common theme),
Yet from this weakness you suppose is due
Sublimer virtue than your Cato knew.
Had Heaven designed us trials so severe,
It would have formed our tempers then to bear.

It is not difficult to guess that the first was written by a man, the second by a woman. The fact that the first sees women from outside, and the second is actually spoken by a woman, is not of course conclusive evidence for this, since there is nothing to stop a poet from speaking through the persona of somebody else – and this is indeed the case in the second passage, which comes from a poem entitled *Epistle from Mrs Y to her Husband*. Mrs Yonge was a real woman, but she is not the author of these lines. She was not a poet, but she was fortunate enough to find a woman to speak for her. That was the only piece of good fortune she had: she ran away from her adulterous husband and took a lover; the husband had her followed and arrested and sued successfully for divorce. He was awarded her dowry and the greater part of her fortune; and most painfully of all, her love letters, some of them very intimate, were read out in open court. As this epistle continues:

But you pursue me to this last retreat.
Dragged into light, my tender crime is shown
And every circumstance of fondness known.
Beneath the shelter of the law you stand,
And urge my ruin with a cruel hand.

Modern readers, male as well as female, will have no difficulty in identifying with Mrs Yonge's shame and anger; and Lady Mary Wortley Montagu's indignant poem makes it clear that at least one woman felt in total sympathy with her. What the men said in the masculine shelter of their clubs we do not know.

Perhaps they said something like what the first passage is saying – though not in verse, and not, of course, so wittily. The sad fate of the old maid is the commonest and among the cruellest of the themes of sexual conflict. If Mrs Yonge had not married her brutal husband, would she have been all that much better off? The contempt with which that first passage treats the beauties who fail to find a husband makes it clear that women are caught between a rock and a hard place.

But is it contempt? Or rather, can we not see contempt as a kind of compassion? Look what they are reduced to, the poem says, and the more painful the state of the old maids, the more relentless the social customs that say 'Husband or nothing', the more it is possible for us to read the savagery of that poem (whether or not this was the poet's purpose in writing it) as an indictment: a picture of the cruelty of social custom, and (therefore) an implicit exposure of a world that gives women only one chance in life. 'I believe single women should have more to do – better chances of interesting and profitable occupation than they possess now': we have no difficulty in identifying that speaker as female, even when she goes on to say 'Existence never was originally meant to be that useless, blank, pale, slow-trailing thing it often becomes to many.' Charlotte Brontë, who put these words into the mind of Caroline Helstone when she felt in danger of never marrying, and gave her a splendidly indignant proto-feminist reflection on the cruelty of society to the old maid, was not tempted to paint the savage picture of the ghosts of beauty that Alexander Pope did. She didn't have – and almost certainly would not have wanted to have – that kind of imagination.

Comparing two passages like these, by a man and by a woman, offers one way into discussing poetry by and about women: what they write is so different – and yet on one level so similar! The authors, Alexander Pope and Lady Mary Wortley Montagu, were not only contemporaries but friends – until they became enemies. After they quarrelled they lampooned one another: Lady Mary pulled no punches:

> If none with vengeance yet thy crimes pursue,
> Or give thy manifold affronts their due;
> If limbs unbroken, skin without a stain,
> Unwhipped, unblanketed, unkicked, unslain,
> That wretched little carcass you retain,
> The reason is, not that the world wants eyes,
> But thou'rt so mean, they see, and they despise.

Hardly ladylike, we might feel, to dwell on Pope's deformities; but Pope was hardly gentlemanlike when he insulted her – though he was more succinct:

> From furious Sappho scarce a milder fate,
> Poxed by her love, or libelled by her hate.

(Contemporary readers can have had little doubt who 'Sappho' was.)

Pope is by common consent the greatest of our 18th century poets; Lady Mary's verse was, until recently, forgotten, or at best remembered as an extra for those who valued her letters or her efforts at introducing vaccination into England. Why? If we look at their *oeuvre*, there is an obvious answer: Pope devoted his life to writing poetry, and the sameness of his versification (always heroic couplets, as the age expected) should not blind us to his range: pastoral, translation of Homer, mock-heroic, *Moral Essays*, imitations of Horace – there is no need to rehearse the details of his brilliant poetic career. In comparison, the verse of Lady Mary looks fragmentary and incidental.

But that, of course, simply confirms the claim that women have been excluded. In a society which confined most women to domestic duties (or, if they were rich enough, to the supervision of domestic duties and the entertaining of men) a career was precisely what a woman could not have. Lady Mary probably did not have to spend much time cooking and cleaning, but that did not necessarily liberate her to be a full-time poet ; both the expectations of society, and the internalising of those expectations, demanded that for her writing verse must be an occasional relaxation, not a serious career.

Familiar, but nonetheless true; but there is one more thing to say, for which we need to look again at our two passages:

> As hags hold Sabbaths, less for joy than spite,
> So these their merry miserable night.
> Still round and round the ghosts of beauty glide
> And haunt the places where their honour died.

We see that this is unkind; we see that the very unkindness strengthens the indignation of the feminist interpreter. But what of the comparison between the old women haunting the dance hall and the witches haunting? This is a wonderful example of what William Empson called an 'equation', in which two meanings of *haunt* are brought together – haunting is what ghosts do, and what people who can't tear themselves away from a place also do. That is brilliant enough, but it is not alone: *gliding round and round* has the same ambiguity, since that is what ghosts do and that is what the women did when they danced in their youth. The old women are real and are also ghosts: they are ridiculous, and also unutterably sad. And the poet can't leave them alone:

> A fop their passion, and their prize a sot;
> Alive ridiculous, and dead forgot.

The lash of contempt is so fiercely intensified by the two contemptuous monosyllables that dismiss the men in their lives as a way of dismissing them, then by dropping the last syllable of 'forgotten', that contempt turns into compassion under our eyes. That, as well as having a career, is what it is to be a poet. How I wish I could find just such brilliance in Lady Mary's verses.

Yet there is brilliance enough. Two lovers who were tenants of Lord Harcourt were struck dead by lightning in 1718, and Pope wrote an epitaph on them:

> When Eastern lovers feed the funeral fire,
> On the same pile the faithful pair expire;
> Here pitying Heaven that virtue mutual found,
> And blasted both, that it might neither wound.
> Hearts so sincere th'Almighty saw well pleased,
> Sent his own lightning, and the victims seized.

Not Pope at his best: a celebration of what looks very like suttee in the first couplet, a confidence about God's intentions that we can hardly be expected to take seriously, the lines seem begging for a cynical rejoinder. Which Lady Mary obligingly provides:

> Here lies John Hughes and Sarah Drew.
> Perhaps you'll say, what's that to you?
> Believe me Friend much may be said
> On this poor couple that are dead.
> On Sunday next they should have married;
> But see how oddly things are carried.
> On Thursday last it rain'd and lighten'd,
> These tender lovers sadly frighten'd
> Shelter'd beneath the cocking Hay
> In hopes to pass the storm away.

But the bold thunder found them out
(Commission'd for that end no doubt)
And seizing on their trembling breath
Consigned them to the shades of death.
Who knows if 'twas not kindly done?
For had they seen the next year's sun
A beaten wife and cuckold swain
Had jointly curs'd the marriage chain.
Now they are happy in their doom
For P. has wrote upon their tomb.

This social condescension can hardly appeal to our democratic senti-
ments; but it is preferable, in many ways, to Pope's pomposity – as
cynicism so often is. One would like to feel that the confident assertion
that their romantic love wouldn't have outlasted the year is a dismissal of
romantic love itself, but it may well, I fear, only be dismissing romance
among the lower orders. More satisfying is the passing scepticism about
providence in the bracketed line – perhaps only because of its succinct-
ness, perhaps because it's a scepticism we're likely to share; and most
satisfying, I suggest, is the final couplet, which does not need to be
changed whether written before or after her quarrel with Pope.

Lady Mary need not be confined too rigorously within the compar-
ison with Pope, so to conclude here are some lines from her Friday
eclogue, in which Lydia (who is now 35) sits in front of her mirror
reflecting on the loss of youth:

What shall I do to spend the hateful day?
At chapel shall I wear the morn away?
Who there appears at these unmodish hours,
But ancient matrons with their frizzled towers,
And grey religious maids? My presence there
Amidst that sober train, would own despair . . .

Does it matter whether the writer was herself a believing Christian – or
whether the reader is? Going to church is here related *only* to age and
lack of lovers, but it is left to us to decide whether that is satire on reli-
gion, or on false religion. The neatest touch, I suggest, is 'unmodish': the
single taken-for-granted term reveals the total subordination of religion
to social function, and distances the speaker from the 'grey religious
maids'. Are they literally grey (church going is for the old), or is *grey reli-
gious* a kind of compound adjective? It is part of the pleasure of poetry

that we do not need to answer such questions, and the poetry reader, in contrast to the biographer, can leave Lady Mary's own beliefs in the ambiguous shadows where, perhaps, she preferred them to remain.

Vile Dependence: Complaints of Marriage

Here are two more lines from the *Epistle from Mrs Y to her Husband*:

> And I prefer this low inglorious state
> To vile dependence on the thing I hate.

Mrs Yonge at least had another man to fly to, though it cost her dear in the end. Most wives, of course, had no alternative, and if saddled with a bad husband had to shrug and bear it. Their one privilege (the word, surely ironical, is Lady Mary's) was to complain, and if they had the gift of being articulate about it (or if they were fortunate enough, like Mrs Yonge, to find a mouthpiece), they could complain in verse. As some did.

> Wife and servant are the same,
> But only differ in the name.
> When she the word *Obey* has said,
> And man by law supreme has made,
> Then all that's kind is laid aside,
> And nothing left but state and pride.

Thus Lady Chudleigh in 1703: the first, not perhaps of many, but of several such complaints. I wish I could be sure what she meant by 'kind'. The sense of 'nature' was normal until the 17th century, for the adjective as well as the noun, and beginning to become obsolete when this poem was written; the modern sense, opposed to 'cruel' or at least to 'indifferent', goes back several centuries before 1703. So Mary Chudleigh could be saying that 'all that's natural' or 'all that's kind (in the modern sense)' was laid aside. The former would of course imply that marriage, or at least patriarchal marriage, was somehow unnatural, and would therefore be much the more radical reading. But we cannot be sure.

Two decades later, Elizabeth Thomas took up the issue:

> From a husband to govern, and buy him his wit:
> From a sullen, ill-natured and whimsical cit: *LIBERA NOS.*

34

In *The True Effigies of a Certain Squire*, Thomas depicts just such a husband, and allows him to speak against his wife's taste for reading: 'for learned ladies are but learned fools.' Hardly a line that is worth dwelling on, but one wonders if he thinks that women are in general less intelligent than men, or if it is their learning that makes them foolish. The 'certain squire' continues:

> Defend me, Fortune, from the wife I hate,
> And let not bookish woman be my fate . . .
> Perhaps you'll say in books you virtue learn,
> And by right reason good from ill discern:
> Ha, ha! Believe me, virtue's but pretence
> To cloak hypocrisy and insolence;
> Let woman mind her economic care,
> And let the man what he thinks fit prepare.

This husband is a boor, seeking to drag down the wife to his own coarse level; but by making him so boorish Thomas leaves it unclear whether he is denouncing learning as such, or learning by women. There is a long tradition of scorn for the blue stocking (that is, the learned or literary woman): it is always unfair, of course, and tends to complain (without evidence) that learned women are merely pedants, literary women merely clumsy versifiers; but it does not necessarily denigrate learning or versifying as such, as this poem appears to. There is a sense in which Elizabeth Thomas is here sinking to the level of her opponents.

A more interesting complaint by the neglected or misunderstood wife is that of Hetty Wright. She was the sister of John Wesley, and must have been an embarrassment to the pious and narrow minded founder of Methodism, though there are signs of ambivalence in his opinion of her. Before her marriage to William Wright she appears to have been what we would call a sexually liberated woman, and what her contemporaries (of course) called a whore. At least two of her poems attack marriage, one of them in outright denunciation:

> Thou source of discord, pain and care,
> Thou sure forerunner of despair,
> Thou scorpion with a double face,
> Thou lawful plague of human race . . .

Here the list of complaints is so general that there seems nothing to establish that a wife is complaining of her husband: it could as easily be read the other way round. More interesting, and more personal, is Wright's *Address to her Husband*:

> O thou, whom sacred rites designed
> My guide and husband, ever kind
> My sovereign master, best of friends,
> On whom my earthly bliss depends;
> If e'er thou didst in Hetty see
> Aught fair or good or dear to thee,
> If gentle speech can ever move
> The cold remains of former love,
> Turn thee at last – my bosom ease,
> Or tell me *why* I cease to please.

The evidence seems uncertain on whether Wright was in fact a bullying or neglectful husband, but that need not matter to us as readers, since plenty of husbands were: the bitter question of this last couplet must have been uttered often enough. We can of course distinguish complaints against the injustice inherent in the institution of marriage, as it then was (material for satire), from laments at the loss of love (material for pathos); the loved husband who cools and turns into a tyrant is material for something more complex than either of these – and more moving. This poem of Hetty Wright's is less interesting when it merely complains (even if the complaints are justified) than when it expresses disappointed puzzlement:

> I oft have wiped these watchful eyes,
> Concealed my cares, and curbed my sighs,
> In spite of grief, to let thee see
> I wore an endless smile for thee.

Mere invective, whether against the institution or the husband, is limited in the scope it gives to poetry; pathos too is limited, but within its limitations it has the power to be moving – at least to the reader (probably female in the 18th century, male or female – we trust – in our own time) who can identify with the wife's position.

All poetry readers know that there are not many new subjects; asking in my introduction how (if at all) women's poetry differs from men's, I wondered whether one possibility might be that it dealt with other subjects. Reading these poems of 18th century women shows us that it sometimes does, and the discovery of a new subject is always liberating.

But what I have not found is a complaint against the husband's cruelty and his power by a wife who still feels the love that drew her to want the marriage in the first place, and therefore still feels divided. That would be more complex, and if well done, more moving; but for that we would need a poem by Dorothea Brooke or Catherine Earnshaw – or Desdemona.

Women against Slavery: Hannah More

After half a century of agitation, the slave trade was abolished by the British government in 1807 (and its anniversary widely celebrated in 2007). When a particular social evil is brought under scrutiny, there will always be a contrast between the moral reformers, protesting against (and horrified by) the iniquities of that institution, and those who point out that it has roots in the structure of society itself, and that its abolition really needs to be preceded by some more fundamental change, the abolition of capitalism or racism or patriarchy or godlessness. On one level, the reformers often succeed when the fundamentalists fail, and the slave trade was abolished in the British Empire, followed 25 years later by the abolition of slavery itself, though capitalism and patriarchy remained more or less undamaged (and godlessness, if anything, increased). The fundamentalists (Marxist, feminist, anti-racist or Christian) will of course reply that not very much has changed, that exploitation, discrimination or sin continues despite superficial institutional changes.

A book on poetry must not expect (or claim) to settle this issue; but ought perhaps to bear it in mind. A book on women's poetry can begin by noticing that most of the women poets of the time wrote anti-slavery poems, all of them reformist: concerned, that is, with the wickedness of that particular institution, rather than seeing it as a consequence of capitalism or patriarchy or even irreligion. The one poet who was herself an ex-slave, Phillis Wheatley, actually expressed her gratitude at having been brought from Africa to America, using an argument often used by defenders of the slave trade:

> 'Twas Mercy brought me from my pagan land,
> Taught my benighted soul to understand
> That there's a God, that there's a Saviour too . . .

No believing Christian could dismiss this argument, but reformers pointed out that the way slaves were treated when brought to America made it clear that saving their souls had not been the motive. Helen Maria Williams pictures the situation of the slave:

> Ah, think how desolate *his* state,
> How *he* the cheerful light must hate,
> Whom, severed from his native soil,
> The morning wakes to fruitless toil,
> To labours hope shall never cheer
> Or fond domestic joy endear . . .

Hannah More paints a lurid picture of how the Africans are captured:

> I see, by more than fancy's mirror shown,
> The burning village and the blazing town,
> See the dire victim torn from social life,
> The shrieking babe, the agonising wife . . .

— and rejects the (often maintained) argument that Negroes do not feel the pains as white people would

> Plead not, in reason's palpable abuse
> Their sense of feeling callous and obtuse,
> From heads to hearts lies nature's plain appeal —
> Though few can reason, all mankind can feel.

— adding a footnote telling us that 'nothing is more frequent than this cruel and stupid argument'.

Anna Barbauld, commiserating with Wilberforce on the rejection of his bill for abolishing the slave trade in 1791, observes

> — Still Africa bleeds,
> Uncheck'd, the human traffic still proceeds.

Charlotte Dacre addresses the issue through narrative, telling the story of 'the poor Negro Sadi' who leaps overboard from a slave ship, manages to swim to a vessel bound for 'Albion's shore', but when he reaches England finds no welcome or sympathy, and dies 'by famine's keen tortures, unaided, alone'. Amelia Opie's ballad, *The Negro Boy's Tale*, was often praised for its pathos: it tells how 'poor Zambo' pleads with 'gentle Anna', daughter of the shipowner, to take him with her from Jamaica to England, where, he has heard, Negro slaves are free, and where, in some confusion, he believes he'll see his mother again. Anna pleads with her father, who at first refuses, then when Zambo leaps overboard, repents, but is too late to save him from drowning. The poem ends:

> Come Justice, come, in glory dressed,
> Oh come, the woe-worn negro's friend,
> The fiend-delighting trade arrest,
> The negro's chains asunder rend.

Isabella Lickbarrow, writing in 1814 when the Napoleonic wars are ending, hopes both for peace in Europe and that other nations may follow Britain's example and protect 'Africa's much-injured sons' from 'the spoiler's hand / And years of slavery – a lingering death.'

It is greatly to the credit of these women poets that they felt driven to take up this cause: that is the first thing to say, and it should not be said patronisingly. After saying it, we can turn to two further questions: did the male poets also write against the slave trade? And how good are these anti-slavery poems?

Of course it is unfair to reproach a poet for the poems he does not write, or to prescribe certain themes as somehow, and for non-poetic reasons, compulsory, or at least expected. So when William Cowper, the most distinguished male poet of the 1780s, in Book V of his long reflective poem *The Task*, which includes reflections on the political institutions of England and France, compares the politics of the two countries, denounces tyranny and, in particular, the Bastille, and contrasts it with English liberty, it is not for readers to complain that he *ought* to mention the slave trade, a disgrace to both countries: there are no 'oughts' in choice of poetic subject. And the fact that Cowper's main point is the 'happy freedom of the man that grace makes free', that he considers religious faith more important than politics, is not a position we can object to poetically, though we may not agree with it politically. But as we read Book V of *The Task*, in which Britain's political institutions are praised, one verbal detail is at least striking. We are loyal to our monarch, but 'not to be his slaves'. English hearts would leap to hear that the Bastille was fallen, that 'our enemies, so oft employ'd / In forging chains for us, themselves were free.' The poet 'could endure / Chains nowhere patiently; and chains at home / Where I am free by birthright, not at all.' Religion is more important than politics because 'He is the freeman, whom the truth makes free, / And all are slaves beside.' How can we help noticing that Cowper loves using the idea of slavery as a metaphor, but does not deal with real slavery? We know that he must have been well aware of it, through his friendship with John Newton, slave-ship captain turned evangelical Christian, but for him slavery remains within the world of discourse, not the real world around him.

And it is no doubt equally unfair to blame a poet for the limitation of her talents: to write a bad poem is a disappointment, but it is not morally culpable. And the admirable anti-slavery poems written by women are all very bad. I take one stanza, to serve for many as example, from *The Poor Negro Sadi*:

> The poor Negro Sadi – what horror befell him,
>   To slavery dragged in the bloom of his years!
> To the food he disdains, the vile lash must compel him –
>   Ah, food doubly bitter when moistened by tears.

The compassion is admirable, the writing deplorable: the clichés ('bloom of his years'), the unnecessary adjectives filling out the metre ('vile lash'), the exclamatory strategy ('what horror befell him'). Stanzas like this make one long for prose, for the simple directness of Olauda Equiano being taken onto a slave ship and wondering 'if we were not to be eaten by those white men, with horrible looks, red faces and loose hair.'

The world is not short of pedestrian or over-written poems, but the versifying on the slave trade can lead one to wonder how we feel about pedestrian poems on an admirable subject. In one way, the subject makes them worse than ever, because our human and political sympathy is being somehow debased. The more worthwhile the subject, the more the poetry-lover can wince, because there's so much more for the poem to spoil.

Probably the best written of these anti-slavery poems is that of Hannah More: the fact that More had no real poetic talent, and wrote with the controlled eloquence of a campaigner, has advantages when it comes to writing such a denunciatory poem, and one line at least is memorable enough to serve as a motto for radical historians: 'Conquest is pillage by a nobler name'.

What, indeed, *is* poetic talent? More is one of the most interesting figures of her time, and she wrote verse, at least in her youth. Her career tells us more about the sensibility of the time than does that of finer poets.

She spent her later life atoning for her literary youth. She didn't quite see it that way, and the change was gradual; but the arch-conservative author of the Cheap Repository Tracts, the patriotic moralist and pious instructor of the poor, must have felt some twinges of embarrassment at her youthful association with blue-stockings and her writing for the stage.

Her poems belong to her youth, but there is enough moralising in them for us to see the continuity with her later self. She was a contemporary of Charlotte Smith, and both are typical of their age: but whereas Smith embodies those elements in 18th century sensibility that lead to the Romantic age, More in later life seems to represent precisely those that don't. Yet it was she who wrote a long poem to Sensibility.

Much of this poem, and of its companion piece, *The Bas-bleu,* or *Conversation,* consists of occasional verse: that is, verse tied to particular people or events, or written for those in the know. These are obviously the least interesting parts today, and only specialists will wish to explore and annotate the references to Mrs Barbauld or David Garrick. The most interesting part of *The Bas-bleu* is its praise of conversation. Who, it asks, would endure the discomforts of foreign travel if 'what he saw must ne'er be known':

> For this he bids his home farewell,
> The joy of seeing is to tell.
> Trust me, he never would have stirred
> Were he forbid to speak a word.

She then contrasts conversation with books ('the mind's food not exercise'), which come to life only when talked about. These reflections about conversation bring the poem to life before it subsides into the dreary abstractions that dominate its later lines: Science and Fancy, Attention, Envy and Wit.

There were frequent arguments about sensibility in the 18th century. Was the sentimentalist, weeping over the sorrows of caged birds or neglected dogs, trivialising suffering, or training our sensibility? was he more or less likely than others to grieve over real suffering and do something about it? Sterne was obsessed by this question, which he explored with brilliant self-consciousness; and More was certainly aware of it.

> Let not the vulgar read this pensive strain,
> Their jests the tender anguish would profane.
> Yet these some deem the happiest of their kind,
> Whose low enjoyments never reached the mind.

Sterne found a model of sentimentality in a servant girl, but for More the vulgar who feel no sensibility are also the vulgar who lack social distinction: a conservative moralist is already lurking in the young woman of letters.

Though the transition between them is smooth, there are two Hannah Mores: the literary young woman, and the pious conservative moralist. Which of them was the author of her poem on slavery?

> Shall Britain, where the soul of Freedom reigns,
> Forge chains for others she herself disdains?
> Forbid it, Heaven! Oh let the nations know
> The liberty she loves she will bestow;
> Not to herself the glorious gift confined,
> She spreads the blessing wide as humankind;
> And scorning narrow views of time and place,
> Bids all be free in earth's extended space.

Those who really wanted slavery abolished would take all the help they could get, and if they did not have quite such a rosy picture of British liberty, would not dissipate their efforts in disowning rhetoric like this: so the poem is radical because it supports the radical cause of abolition. But who can deny the smugness of lines like these, confident that Britain has achieved freedom, and needs only a rhetorical push to give it to the world. Working-class radicals in the 19th century often complained that the abolitionists were more interested in the welfare of black men they had never set eyes on than in the unsanitary poverty on their own doorstep. Such people did not care for Hannah More.

Charlotte Smith

Perhaps the most striking feature of Charlotte Smith's poetry is how very literary it is. She is well-read in English poetry, likes to point this out, and quotes freely from other poets. Writing a sonnet to Hope, she ends it:

> 'For me the vernal garland blooms no more'.
> Come then, 'pale Misery's love', be thou my cure,
> And I will bless thee, who though slow art sure.

The first line is by Pope; 'pale Misery's love' is a quotation from Shakespeare. Writing a sonnet 'On the Departure of the Nightingale', she regrets that it will be long before 'thou shalt . . . pour thy music on the "night's dull ear"', and declares 'The pensive muse shall own thee for her mate'. 'Night's dull ear' is from Shakespeare, the muse calls the nightingale her mate in Milton's first sonnet. There is no attempt to conceal these borrowings: the quotations are put in inverted commas, so that we'll realise they are quotations. Several of the sonnets are 'from Petrarch', several are attributed to Goethe's Werther. Other poets are mentioned and complimented – contemporaries of Smith's who shared her taste for sentimentality and for nature, some of them totally forgotten: writing to the Naiad of the Sussex river Arun, she lists other Sussex poets who have 'raised thy glory high', including one John Sargent, who has not even found his way into the *DNB*, and who owes his tiny glimmer of fame only to Charlotte Smith's goodwill.

We probably associate such self-conscious literariness with the sophistications of modernism, but it can of course be naïve rather than sophisticated, a sign not that literature feeds on itself, as in, say, Ezra Pound, but rather that the poet is a modest member of a profession, assuming that her readers are pleased to be instructed.

Smith's *Elegiac Sonnets*, published in 1784, were described by her as beguiling some very melancholy moments by expressing them in verse. Melancholy was a favourite topic of 18th century verse, so it is difficult to know whether Smith's sonnets are better regarded as conventional examples of 18th century melancholy, or as anticipations of the Romantic odes to Dejection and Melancholy. The first generation of Romantics knew and admired Charlotte Smith's poetry, and it seems natural to compare her with Wordsworth. Both, for instance, wrote sonnets to Sleep – which, like most sonnets to sleep, are actually about insomnia:

> Come, balmy sleep, tired nature's soft resort,
> On these sad temples all thy poppies shed,
> And bid gay dreams from Morpheus' airy court
> Float in light vision round my aching head . . .

> A flock of sheep that leisurely pass by,
> One after one; the sound of rain, and bees
> Murmuring; the fall of rivers, winds and seas,
> Smooth fields, white sheets of water, and pure sky;
> I have thought of all by turns . . .

Neither poem is a masterpiece, but Wordsworth's certainly emerges as the more immediate. Whereas Smith begins with a conventional invocation and mythological allusion (and continues with a reminiscence of Shakespeare), he begins with a very matter-of-fact description of insomnia: *leisurely* is a particularly vivid touch, capturing his annoyance

43

at futilely counting sheep that take no notice of him. Smith is more impressive when more intense, and perhaps the best of her sonnets is 'On Being Cautioned against Walking on an Headland Overlooking the Sea, because it was Frequented by a Lunatic':

> Is there a solitary wretch who hies
>   To the tall cliff, with starting pace or slow,
> And, measuring, views with wild and hollow eyes
>   Its distance from the waves that chide below;
> Who, as the sea-born gale with frequent sighs
>   Chills his cold bed upon the mountain turf,
> With hoarse, half-uttered lamentation, lies
>   Murmuring responses to the dashing surf?
> In moody sadness on the giddy brink,
>   I see him more with envy than with fear;
> *He* has no *nice felicities* that shrink
>   From giant horrors, wildly wandering here,
> He seems (uncursed with reason) not to know
>   The depth or the duration of his woe.

The long-winded title was perhaps necessary to allow the poem to begin with a question, as if responding to what she has just been told about the lunatic. The first eight lines repeat (or imagine) what she has learnt, then the sestet (much the most striking part of the poem) offers a personal comment in the grimly matter of fact 'I see him more with envy than with fear'; and culminates in the chilling last line, whose alliteration seems to capture the poet's attempt to understand, from the outside, what can only be known from within.

Smith's most serious and most ambitious poem also invites comparison with Wordsworth. *The Emigrants* is a poem in blank verse about the priests and aristocrats who fled from France when the massacres began. Because Smith and her husband had fled to France to avoid his creditors, she is able to write 'I too have known Involuntary exile' and

> Have felt how sad
> It is to look across the dim cold sea
> That melancholy rolls its refluent tides
> Between us and the dear regretted land . . .

Both Wordsworth and Smith began as enthusiasts for the French Revolution, and then turned from it in revulsion when the massacres began. So much powerful poetry has been written from outside, by poets who only imagined what war or revolution were like, that it is salutary to realise that actually being present does give an irreplaceable advantage. Smith did not, as Wordsworth did, find herself at a village festival where liberty was being celebrated in 1790, and so she could not have written the most famous lines ever inspired by the revolution:

> Bliss was it in that dawn to be alive,
> But to be young was very Heaven . . .

Her revulsion from the Terror, too, has not the immediacy of Wordsworth's imagining of the massacres when he stood in the Square of the Carrousel and thought about what had happened, and 'The fear gone by Pressed on me almost like a fear to come' – though even there, we can notice, Wordsworth, always the 'spectator ab extra', was not actually present at the massacres. It is not easy to say what makes Wordsworth's sense of horror so much more powerful than Smith's outrage when she thinks of Marat ('a wretch whose private vice Makes even the wildest profligate recoil, And who . . . has burst The laws of nature and humanity'). His distance from the Terror itself seems just right for his poem – close enough to shudder with real not rhetorical horror, far enough to be imagining it.

Smith is a minor poet compared to Wordsworth, but we can ask what she offers that he can't. Puzzled by finding on the Downs 'the strange and foreign forms / Of seashells', though she is sure that the blue Ocean 'here never rolled its surge', she wonders:

> Does Nature then
> Mimic in wanton mood, fantastic shapes
> Of bivalves and inwreathed volutes that cling
> To the dark sea-rock of the wat'ry world?
> Or did this range of chalky mountains once
> Form a vast basin where the ocean waves
> Swelled fathomless . . .

Smith does not really believe that Nature is an Entity, or 'the nurse, the guide Of all my moral being', as Wordsworth's Nature is, but she sees it as something much more like the scientist's nature: a word for what actually happens. The questions she asks about natural history are more like real questions than rhetorical gestures, and her habit of adding footnotes to her poem, spelling out some of the natural history, sometimes charming, sometimes irritating, here seems very apt:

Among the crumbling chalk I have often found shells, some quite in a fossil state and hardly distinguishable from chalk. Others appeared more recent – cockles mussels and periwinkles, I well remember, were among the number, and some whose names I did not know. A great number were like those of small land-snails. It is now many years since I made these observations . . .

The matter-of-fact honesty of a note like this adds a kind of penumbra of honesty to the poem itself, offering a contrast to the sublime egoism of Wordsworth.

Romanticism & Politics

Two poets sat down in the 1790s to write a political poem fiercely critical of the existing social order. One was Mary Robinson, a much-painted beauty (both by Romney and by Reynolds), briefly the mistress of the Prince of Wales, almost as briefly the darling of the London stage (from which came her nickname Perdita) and author of several books of poems – largely forgotten until recently. Her poem is called *The Birth-Day*:

> Here bounds the gaudy, gilded chair,
>   Bedecked with fringe and tassels gay;
> The melancholy mourner there
>   Pursues her sad and painful way.
>
> Here, guarded by a motley train,
>   The pampered Countess glares along;
> There, wrought by poverty and pain,
>   Pale misery mingles with the throng.

How is a radical poem to confront power relations? In theory, it should not be difficult to devise an answer: it will set exploiter and exploited against each other in a series of contrasts, and if it is (for instance) in quatrains, it can follow two lines about the rich with two lines about the poor, clinching each contrast by the rhyme. If the aim is to excite indignation, the poor will regard the rich with envy and longing, and the rich will regard the poor with indifference and disdain ('disdain', in fact, will make a good rhyme word: so does 'sigh' – rhyming with 'tearful eye' or 'grief' – with 'craving relief'). A series of stanzas based on this simple

contrast may have a cumulative force, or may begin to sound monoto-
nous: monotony, after all, is the flip side of cumulative insistence, and a
poem attacking the social order needs to strike blow after similar blow.

> Here, amidst jewels, feathers, flowers,
> The senseless Duchess sits demure,
> Heedless of all the anguished hours
> The sons of modest worth endure.

As the poem nears its end the pace can be slowed and the poor brought
more into the centre; they could be allowed a whole stanza, even two,
and the rich could be relegated to the function of not noticing.

And how should such a poem end? We would expect some kind of
reversal – not perhaps a successful revolution (unless the poet is very
confident of a political solution) but at least a threat, or a questioning of
the status quo. This, as the reader will have realised, is more or less the
poem that Mary Robinson wrote: five stanzas begin 'Here' – referring to
the rich – and three of them balance it with 'there' in line 3. In stanza 5
the lacqueys shout 'Stand back ' and the wretched poor 'are driven
around'; they scattered fly 'And shrink before the threatening sound.' In
stanza 7 we encounter the Duchess:

> All silvered and embroidered o'er
> She neither knows nor pities pain;
> The beggar, freezing at her door
> She overlooks with nice disdain.

And in the eleventh and last stanza, the Duchess will get her comup-
pance:

> 'Take physic, pomp!' let Reason say:
> 'What can avail thy trappings rare?
> The tomb shall close thy glittering day,
> The beggar prove thy equal there.

Duchess and beggar will be equal in the tomb. This is of course a poetic
commonplace: the glories of our blood and state are shadows not substan-
tial things; but if regarding them as shadows is the price of continuing to
enjoy them, the rich and the powerful will be quite willing to pay it.
Beggar and duchess will be equal in death – but not till then. So it is not,
after all, a radical poem: Death the Leveller poems never are.

Mary Robinson's poem is very well-behaved: metrically, structurally – and politically. Its generous indignation is subversive neither of the norms of poetic discourse nor of the social structure. Are we then to conclude that poems with regular metre and logical arrangement are politically conservative?

The other radical poet who wrote about the state of England at the same time – also in quatrains – was William Blake.

> I wander through each charter'd street
> Near where the charter'd Thames does flow,
> And mark in every face I meet
> Marks of weakness, marks of woe.

The metre is regular – even insistent; but the arrangement is not nearly as logical, or as univocal, as it might seem, or as it was in Mary Robinson. That repeated *charter'd* sounds angry, and also draws attention to the way the meaning has shifted: a charter can be a stuffy old document that grants privileges and restrictions, or it can be a new document that offers freedom, so in the very first line that poem seems to invite contrasting readings: London is a place where everything is regulated, even the river; or, London is liberated by a charter which was granted to every street – even to the river, and so means nothing. Two readings: both indignant.

What of the third stanza?

> How the Chimney-sweeper's cry
> Every blackening church appalls,
> And the hapless soldier's sigh
> Runs in blood down palace walls.

'Appalls' can mean 'shocks' or it can mean 'casts a pall over'; a church is both an institution and a building; *black'ning* can be active or passive. As an institution, the church blackens the moral scene; as a building it grows blacker, from the soot shed by the chimney sweeper. The soldier, too, is an ambiguous figure: is he a deserter being shot, or (a subtler reading, surely) a reluctant trooper crushing a riot – in both cases the charter'd streets are the scene of oppression.

There is much more to explore in Blake's poem, but it should be clear by now that it is radical in two senses. It is filled with indignation against the social order, and it subverts our demand for clarity, since the meaning offered constantly shifts into something else. Is the political impact of the poem strengthened or weakened by this verbal subversion? If we describe both these effects as radical, are we indulging in the same kind of verbal shifting as the poem?

The commonsense answer will say yes, we are: that the verbal uncertainty obviously weakens the radicalism. The more we are thrown into linguistic confusion – or into the pleasure of sorting out what looked like confusion – the more we are distracted from the political message: does the poet want us to enjoy his skill, or to rally to his cause? But the view that the really radical act is to undermine our confidence in the clear statements that enable society to function – the view often put forward by Roland Barthes – will claim 'that which is paradoxical, that which cannot be brought within good sense', will always be liberating; that the really radical act is to reject the 'va-sans-dire', which is a form of totalitarianism. So will a truly radical poem need or despise coherence?

I doubt if this issue can be settled by argument, but I will try. The function of real radicalism is to replace the oppressive elements in society by something better, and this programme needs clarity just as much as the conservative programme does. The radicals need to know where they are going. So it is quite arguable that the linguistic subversion Blake is indulging in has a conservative function, since it inhibits rational exploration of alternatives to the status quo. But it is perhaps better to argue that it is non-political. The conservative reader of *London* can delight in the poetry and regard the radicalism with a tolerant smile; the radical reader can delight in the poetry *and* in the subversion, and forget, while reading, the task of translating radical indignation into a programme. The poetry-loving reader can become a kind of provisional radical, suspending the question how the poem affects his political attitudes; that would be the 'willing suspension of disbelief that constitutes poetic faith.'

But has this whole comparison been unfair to Mary Robinson as a poet? She wrote another satiric poem that is both very similar to and very different from *The Birthday*:

> Pavements slippery, people sneezing,
> Lords in ermine, beggars freezing;
> Tired gluttons dainties carving,
> Genius in a garret starving . . .
> Arts and sciences bewailing;
> Commerce drooping, credit failing;
> Placemen mocking subjects loyal;
> Separations, weddings royal . . .
> Poets, painters, and musicians;
> Lawyers, doctors, politicians:

> Pamphlets, newspapers and odes,
> Seeking fame by different roads.

This poem flaunts its structure even more ostentatiously than *The Birthday*, but it is not the same structure: it uses the simple, the deliberately crude strategy of omitting the verbs and offering a series of noun phrases, most of them noun followed by a present participle, sometimes by a past participle to show the passivity of the noun ('youthful damsels quite forsaken'), sometimes by an adjective to suggest the inevitability with which it belongs to its noun ('lordlings empty and insipid'), sometimes just a string of nouns to suggest that one sees them everywhere ('Pamphlets, newspapers and odes'). What is the cumulative effect of this? It is, surely, to suggest the helplessness of everyone and everything, all caught up in the same swirl of syntax, all reduced to a list of examples of what is going on around us and we can do nothing to alter. 'Like it or not, that's what there is,' says the syntax. 'Everywhere.'

Structurally, the poem is as crude as *The Birthday*, but instead of seeming more and more obvious as it continues, it seems more and more inevitable, in order to show us how helpless we all are, caught up in the swirl with which we all fit into our predictable roles. It turns the limitations of its technique into its own satiric impact.

Almost twenty years later a very different radical poem was published. *Eighteen Hundred and Eleven*, by Anna Letitia Barbauld, is an explicitly political poem, especially interesting for us to read as a reminder of what it must have felt like when Napoleon was winning. It begins with an account of Napoleon's tyranny, resisted 'bravely, though vainly' by Britain. It tells us, in often very competent heroic couplets, that Freedom has been defeated:

> Prostrate she lies beneath the Despot's sway,
> While the hushed nations curse him – and obey.

Though it looks at first as if the poem is going to praise Britain's heroic resistance, it soon becomes clear that it is an attack on war itself: Nature 'clothes with corn the vale' but

> Man calls to Famine, nor invokes in vain,
> Disease and Rapine follow in her train.

Then come lines on the mother who loses her sons in war, a common enough theme in political poems, which can either praise the mother for her willingness to sacrifice in a fine cause, or pity her for her loss; and this poem only does the second. The mother pores over the map,

> Asks *where* the spot that wrecked her bliss is found,
> And learns its name but to detest the sound.

The shift from attacking Napoleon to attacking war becomes quite explicit:

> Britain, know,
> Thou who hast shared the guilt must share the woe.

For the patriotic reader, worse – much worse – is to come: the poem then looks into the future, and suggests that it may be Britain's fate 'To rank among the names that once were great', providing the authors who will be read in the New World, while American visitors come to look at the once great sights in Britain. This took a century or two, but it has now happened; the poem anticipates the modern tourist trade almost uncannily. The British host

> To every spot shall lead his wondering guests
> On whose known site the beam of glory rests:
> Here Chatham's eloquence in thunder broke,
> Here Fox persuaded, or here Garrick spoke . . .

– all that is missing is the paid tourist guide!

This was too much for conservative reviewers. The poem was savagely attacked, not on poetic but on political grounds, and the Tory *Quarterly Review* described it as a 'party pamphlet in verse'. There cannot be many such clear examples of a poem being condemned by contemporaries for precisely the qualities that could commend it to later ages. Though our feelings on the subject may vary, few today deny, and fewer still would consider it unpatriotic to mention, that Britain is no longer one of the world's great powers.

And its merits as a poem? It is not writing bad poetry that gets poets into trouble, it is writing poetry – good or bad – with the wrong sentiments. Indeed, one reader considered *Eighteen Hundred and Eleven* 'only the more dangerous on account of its poetical excellence'. It does indeed have poetical excellence, but we need to notice of what kind. By 1811, Blake had heard the voice of the Bard, and had published a great deal that was quite as subversive as *London*. Coleridge had written

Kubla Khan and *The Ancient Mariner*, Wordsworth had written the Lucy poems and a draft of *The Prelude*: we are in the middle of what literary historians think of as the Romantic movement, a movement which *London* obviously belongs to. As poetry, *Eighteen Hundred and Eleven* shows total unawareness of all that: Mrs Barbauld had almost certainly never read Blake, and stylistically her poem could have been written before Wordsworth and Coleridge were born. Politically radical it may be, attacked it may have been by conservative critics, but poetically it is not in the least radical. Like most, perhaps all, of the women's poetry of the turn of the century (including Mary Robinson's) it is poetically conservative.

Eighteen Hundred and Eleven seems to me Barbauld's most interesting poem, even though it ended her career as a poet. Time, on the whole, has not dealt kindly with her. Readers of Coleridge's *Ancient Mariner* often come across her objection that the poem has no moral, and remembering its trite stanza about 'The dear God that loveth us / He made and loveth all' are likely to agree with Coleridge that it has too much moral, and classify Barbauld (rather unfairly) as a moraliser. And her poem on *The Rights of Woman* will not commend her to posterity. It begins 'Yes, injured woman! rise, assert thy right!'; but that rousing first line turns out to be a mocking summary of Mary Wollstonecraft's *Vindication,* and the poem ends by informing the crusading woman that 'separate rights are lost in mutual love' – the riposte of thousands of conservative husbands to the crusading feminist. Barbauld held some liberal views, but not about women's rights.

Surprisingly, perhaps, for so earnest a woman, she wrote some comic poems, of which her mock-heroic account of *Washing Day* is perhaps the most successful. Since she was an accomplished versifier (we can see this from the half-dozen songs she wrote), it is surprising that she wrote it in blank verse: perhaps we are over-influenced by the polish of Pope's *Rape of the Lock*, but there is an expectation that the mock-heroic achieves some of its best effects through turning its polished versification to comic use, and *Washing-Day* foregoes the chance to do this. All the same, it is livelier and more interesting than a good deal of burlesque verse, and some of its lines seem to me really memorable, like 'And all the petty miseries of life', or this childhood reminiscence:

> At intervals my mother's voice was heard,
> Urging dispatch: briskly the work went on,
> All hands employed to wash, to rinse, to wring,
> To fold, and starch, and clap, iron, and plait.

Then I would sit me down and ponder much
What washings were.

Lists of verbs are so much more interesting than lists of adjectives.

Barbauld's most popular poem, during her lifetime, was *The Mouse's Petition to Doctor Priestley Found in the Trap where he had been confined all Night*. It is hard to be quite sure of its tone.

If e'er thy breast with freedom glowed,
And spurned a tyrant's chain,
Let not thy strong oppressive force
A free-born mouse detain . . .

The well-taught philosophic mind
To all compassion gives;
Casts round the world an equal eye,
And feels for all that lives.

Joseph Priestley, the discoverer of oxygen, was both a distinguished scientist and a man of radical political views. Barbauld knew and admired him: he had encouraged her to write poetry, and she would certainly have believed that he did have a 'well-taught philosophic mind'; the fact that the mouse uses his own arguments must be a form of teasing rather than of real mockery. Legend has it that Priestley released the mouse – though since he was using mice to experiment on, he no doubt caught another. Priestley himself wrote 'it is paying dear for philosophical' [that is, scientific] 'discoveries, to purchase them at the expense of humanity', but he did not take this apology seriously enough to suspend his experiments. Neither of them can have dreamt that the dispute about animal experiments would become so much more violent two hundred years later: a light-hearted poem can turn sour when read in a later, more combative age.

Note   Roger Lonsdale's splendid anthology *Eighteenth Century Women Poets* (Oxford 1989) contains many, though not all, of the poems discussed in this chapter, and is certainly the best collection of relevant texts. Anne Finch's *Selected Poems* is edited by Katherine M. Rogers (1979). Lady Mary Wortley Montagu's *Essays and Poems* (with *Simplicity, a Comedy)* is a Clarendon Paperback (Oxford 1993). The lines by Pope beginning 'Pleasures the sex' are from his 3rd *Moral Essay ('On the Character of Women')*. All the poems quoted in 'Vile Dependence' are in Lonsdale's anthology, as are those against slavery.

A modern edition of *The Poems of Anna Letitia Barbauld* is published by the University of Georgia Press (Athens & London, 1994) and one of *The Poems of Charlotte Smith* by Oxford University Press, 1993. Roland Barthes' views as cited in the discussion of satire and romanticism can most conveniently be explored in *Roland Barthes par Roland Barthes* (Seuil: Paris, 1980) or in *Roland Barthes: Image – Music – Text* (ed. by Stephen Heath, Fontana, 1977).

3

The Nineteenth Century

The Breaking Heart: Mrs Hemans and L.E.L.

> Ah, dearly purchased is the gift,
> The gift of song like thine;
> A fated doom is hers who stands
> The priestess of the shrine.
> The crowd – they only see the crown,
> They only hear the hymn; –
> They mark not that the cheek is pale,
> And that the eye is dim.

The sentiment of these lines is a common one, that poetry has its origin in suffering, and the public who enjoy the poems don't realise this. They were written by Letitia Elizabeth Landon about Felicia Hemans, but she must also have been thinking of herself. These were the two most popular woman poets in early 19th century England, perhaps the two most popular English woman poets ever. Landon is quite forgotten today; Hemans is remembered for *Casablanca,* her poem in praise of obedience. By a quirk of survival, its opening lines have become one of the quotations that 'everyone knows': 'The boy stood on the burning deck / Whence all but he had fled' – though few of those who know these two lines could name the author, and fewer still could continue the quotation (it continues 'The flame that lit the battle's wreck / Shone round him o'er the dead'). The point of the poem is to praise the obstinate courage of the boy who would not leave his post until his father gave him leave, but since the father lay 'faint in death below' the boy stuck to his post and was 'the noblest thing that perished there'. A poem in praise of duty – or, to put it differently, in praise of the stupidity of obedience.

The morality of Hemans' poems, as of her life, is exemplary and conventional. She was devoted to her mother and her four sons, and never reproached the husband who walked out on her; the poems praise piety, duty, heroism and the family. The opening of one of her poems has passed into the language:

> The stately homes of England,
>   How beautiful they stand!
> Amidst their tall ancestral trees,
>   O'er all the pleasant land.
> The deer across their greensward bound
>   Through shade and sunny gleam,
> And the swan glides past them with the sound
>   Of some rejoicing stream.

It is perhaps brutal to expose the conventional poems of an outmoded taste to the cool gaze of a later age, which will notice – and censure – all the obvious 'poetic' devices: the exclamatory sentences (as in the second line), the archaisms (*amidst, o'er, sward*), the predictable adjectives (*ancestral* trees) or verbs (the deer *bound*) or even nouns (*deer* and *swan*). The policy of this book is to discuss the poets I admire and ignore the bad ones: there are always more bad poets than good, both male and female. But to ignore Felicia Hemans would have seemed perverse, since she was the most successful and (when alive) the most admired of all women poets in the language, and must at least be mentioned.

Landon (L.E.L., as she was always known) seems to me more interesting than Hemans, since she is a kind of monument to the belief that a female poet should be talented, beautiful, passionate (but sexually restrained), if possible Italian, and able to improvise in front of large audiences. The model for this was Corinne, heroine of Mme de Stael's sensationalist and very popular novel. It is difficult to read *Corinne* with any enthusiasm today, but it was enormously influential, and L.E.L.'s first success was a book of poems called *l'Improvisatrice*, in which an Italian poetess – a carbon copy of Corinne – makes up stories about women betrayed in love. L.E.L. did not improvise, but her poems read as though she did, and her gift for fluent versifying suggests that she could have. She was not Italian but several of her heroines were.

As well as Corinne, the model behind L.E.L. was Sappho, and the one poem of hers that is still faintly remembered is called *Sappho's Song*: it too connects poetry with suffering:

> Farewell, my lute! – and would that I
>   Had never waked thy burning chords!
> Poison has been upon thy sigh

> And fever has breathed in thy words . . .
> It was my evil star above,
>> Not my sweet lute, that wrought me wrong;
> It was not song that taught me love,
>> But it was love that taught me song.

Those last two lines could be a kind of apology for everything she wrote: the claim that her emotions are not factitious, not manufactured for the sake of writing poetry, but are the true origin of the poems, is of course a Romantic commonplace: its most famous statement is Shelley's:

>> Most wretched men
> Are cradled into poetry by wrong.
> They learn in suffering what they teach in song.

– a passage which L.E.L no doubt knew.

To read these two women is to be shown two versions of the taste of a past age, which is always historically interesting even if we feel grateful that it is no longer our taste, and decide that that they deserve to be forgotten. It is not my aim to suggest that they should be remembered; but I must add that that is the aim of a powerful current in recent academic study, the feminist criticism of the texts of the Romantic movement. This movement embodies two contrasting claims, a contrast that inevitably besets feminist literary study: on the one hand, the claim that the inferiority of women's poetry at this (or any other) period shows how patriarchal society has oppressed women, how its limited estimation of feminine powers became a self-fulfilling prophecy, so that women wrote all too conventional and forgettable poetry because they were expected to; and on the other hand, that their poems are not at all inferior or forgettable, but have been dismissed because of the prejudices of the male taste-makers. Both these positions are so attractive to the feminist critic that it is not surprising that there have been attempts to combine them, incompatible though they may seem.

To pursue this discussion would bring us to the dilemma that I looked at briefly in the Introduction: My aim is to discuss poems rather than literary theory, but to defend this decision inevitably involves discussing literary theory. So I shall refer the interested reader to the feminist discussions of Romanticism (for which see the note), and add one further remark that will fit Landon into literary history.

The two leading women poets of Victorian England, Elizabeth Browning and Christina Rossetti, both knew the work of L.E.L. (that is not surprising) and both, as it happens, wrote a poem about her. At the age of 36 L.E.L. unexpectedly married the governor of Cape Coast castle in West Africa and went to live there, but died soon after arriving; this unleashed speculation about whether the death was accident, suicide or murder, all of which added fascination to her reputation. On the voyage out she wrote two poems to the English friends she had left behind, one of which contains the refrain

> My friends, my absent friends!
> Do you think of me as I think of you?

Elizabeth Browning, her attention caught by the pathos of this question – the fact that L.E.L., leaving England, thought not of her fame but of her need for love – and by the sadness of her dying before she could receive an answer, wrote a sad poem called 'L.E.L.'s Last Question':

> None smile and none are crowned where lieth she,
> With all her visions unfulfilled save one,
> Her childhood's, of the palm-tree in the sun . . .

Christina Rossetti's attention was caught not only by Landon's refrain but also by Browning's poem, and for her, too, Landon became a figure of pure pathos: she headed her poem 'L.E.L. Whose heart was breaking for a little love', and repeated that line as a refrain in every stanza. And this can suggest why we need not grieve at the fact that Hemans and Landon have lost their once great fame; if we grant to Hemans and Landon the once dominant place they held among women poets, we are in danger of admitting only one subject for women's poetry, pathos; and of drawing into their orb two far greater poets – both of whom, fortunately, are more complex and more interesting.

Note   The poems of Hemans (but not of Landon) can still be found – very cheap – in second-hand bookshops; and generous selections from both are printed in Duncan Wu's anthology of Romantic Woman Poets, or in other anthologies cited in the note attached to my Introduction. For an introduction to modern feminist academic discussion of woman Romantic poets, see *Romanticism and Feminism,* edited by Anne K. Mellor (Indiana University Press), which contains both theoretical essays and an invaluable discussion of women poets of the period – with ample quotation – by Stuart Curran.

The Brownings

If we had set out to design an experiment that would tell us as much as possible about how men and how women write about love, we could not have invented anything better than the Brownings. They wrote the fullest and most eloquent love letters in existence, all of which have been preserved; they eloped and lived happily ever after; they were both distinguished poets, and they wrote love poems both fictional and autobiographical, both of them at times using the persona of the other sex. We can therefore compare the male and the female poet writing of love; the man writing as a woman and the woman writing as a man; and the directness of a love letter with the indirections of poetry, asking which gives the truer picture of the experience of being in love (or asking what we mean by 'truer'). What more could we ask for?

Elizabeth wrote the Sonnets from the Portuguese during 1846 and 1847 (some of them at least before they married), showed them to Robert in 1847, printed them privately in that year, and included them in her works three years later. Why 'from the Portuguese'? The device of passing off such very personal poems as translations is a fairly obvious strategy of modesty; the poems use many of the conventions of the love poetry of the troubadours, but to call them 'Sonnets from the Provençal' would have seemed misleading to readers familiar with the work of Geoffroi Rudel or Bertrand de Ventadour; originally they were to be called 'Sonnets from the Bosnian', but this must have seemed, on reflection, too remote for credibility. Portuguese is a Romance language which readers are unlikely to know but might expect that so learned a poet would; and which might well contain love poems in the medieval tradition – poems like this:

> Unlike are we, unlike, O princely Heart!
> Unlike our uses and our destinies.
> Our ministering two angels look surprise
> On one another, as they strike athwart
> Their wings in passing. Thou, bethink thee, art
> A guest for queens to social pageantries,
> With gages from a hundred brighter eyes
> Than tears even can make mine, to play thy part

Of chief musician. What hast thou to do
With looking from the lattice lights at me,
A poor, tired, wandering singer, singing through
The dark, and leaning up a cypress tree?
The chrism is on thine head, – on mine, the dew, –
And death must dig the level where these agree.

It is a familiar situation: the lover serenading out of the darkness, leaning upon a cypress tree, looking up literally (the beloved is at an upstairs window or on a balcony) and emotionally (he regards her with awe), perhaps even socially (the minstrel sings to a lady of high degree – 'a guest to queens'). He? Of course it's a he, as it always is in the poetry of courtly love: the poet offers worship to the woman whom he regards with religious awe, comparing her to an angel, even (in Dante) to the Virgin Mary, begging for a glance from her bright eyes. (That such idealisation takes place in patriarchal society should not, of course, surprise us; it can serve the function of reconciling women to their powerless lot by offering them a semblance of power.)

But in this case the poet is a she, the beloved is a he. The fact is not concealed from readers, who as well as picking up the occasional gendered detail ('I never gave a lock of hair away / To a man, dearest, except this to thee') will have seen the poet's Christian name, Elizabeth, on the title page. Reading this sonnet with conventional expectations we notice immediately that the sexes are reversed, and that makes it quite a different poem. The poet is not shut out from the social pageantries because of being a minstrel of lower social standing, but because of being a woman: women don't get invited to male parties – or, if we want to be even more biographical, because this woman was a semi-invalid, and stayed home in the evening when Robert went out to enjoy his social life. The chrism is no longer a metaphor to indicate the social superiority of the beloved; it can be read more literally as saying 'You are a more distinguished poet than I am' (though in 1847 Robert wasn't: it must be a compliment, not a statement of fact). We can go so far as to say that we have here two poems, identical in wording, but with quite different meanings, depending on the context we provide for them: the context of literary tradition to which the title invites us, or that of the 19th century society to which we know that the poet actually belonged.

To bring in the real live author of the poems, we can naturally turn to the abundant material we possess: the love letters. The sonnet which most clearly overlaps with, or at least draws, on these is probably no. 20:

Belovéd, my belovéd, when I think
That thou wast in the world a year ago,
What time I sat alone here in the snow
And saw no footprint, heard the silence sink
No moment at thy voice, but, link by link,
Went counting all my chains as if that so
They never could fall off at any blow
Struck by thy possible hand, – why, thus I drink
Of life's great cup of wonder! Wonderful,
Never to feel thee thrill the day or night
With personal act of speech, – nor ever call
Some prescience of thee with the blossoms white
Thou sawest growing! Atheists are as dull,
Who cannot guess God's presence out of sight.

Elizabeth's letters are far more occupied than Robert's with looking back at the time before they knew each other, which she does with a kind of shudder (she even uses the word):

Observe how, if I had died in this illness, I should have left a sealed world behind me! you, unknown too – unguessed at, you, in many respects, wonderfully unguessed at! this . . . the last revelation, unread! How the thought of it used to depress me sometimes. (2 March 1846)

Nearly a year ago! How the time passes! If I had 'done my duty' like the enchanted fish leaping on the gridiron, and seen you never again after that first visit, you would have forgotten all about me by this day. Or at least 'that prude' I should be! (30 March 1846)

I shudder to look back to the days when you were not for me. Was ever life so like death before? My face was so close to the tombstones that there seemed no room even for the tears. (4 June)

The central thought of the sonnet, the astonishment with which she now looks back on a time when she did not know him, derives straight from the letters: 'wonderfully unguessed at' has turned into 'Wonderful, Never to feel thee thrill the day or night', and the consciousness of being blindfolded when she did not yet know what sight was going to come to her, has turned into the negative so brilliantly presented as a positive in 'thy possible hand'.

What, then, has happened to the material of the letters when it turns into a poem – apart from the obvious fact of versification? There is a restriction of register: in the flexibility of a letter she can move with ease from 'the sevenfold Heaven' to the 'enchanted fish' to 'that prude', but in the formality of a poem she cannot get too far away from 'Beloved my beloved'. Whereas the phrasing of the letters says 'This is for you only', that of the poem says 'This is addressed to the one I love', in a manner that invites the reader to apply it to the one he (or she) loves. The basic difference between a poem and a letter is, after all, that a letter has a recipient, whereas a poem is addressed to anyone who reads it.

But the most striking change is found, surely, in the last couplet of the poem. Would she ever, in a letter, have compared Robert to God? Not even the strongest Victorian exhortations to wifely submission, whether from Ruskin or Mrs Ellis, quite propose that; but it does not seem out of place in the heightened rhetoric of the sonnet (where it can after all be excused as an analogy, not an assertion).

The Christian is exhorted both to worship God and to love God. Are these the same? Loving God might go with worshipping God, but does human love require you to worship the beloved? This is a question raised over and over in the letters, both by Robert and by Elizabeth. She asks (17 June '46) 'Why did you love me, my beloved, when you might have chosen from the most perfect of all women, and each would have loved you with the perfectest of her nature?' or she begs (18 June) 'Dearest and ever dearest, try to forgive me when I fall so manifestly short of you in all things.' He says (6 July) 'You give me a jewel . . . I am not worthy of any gift, you must know.' It is he who theorises this habit by declaring (10 Aug.) 'There is no love but from beneath, far beneath, – that is the law of its nature' – a view she protests against, though there is no real disagreement between them, since if each looks up to the other a kind of equality is established. Turned into a poem, this becomes:

> And as a vanquished soldier yields his sword
> To one who lifts him from the bloody earth,
> Even so, Beloved, I at last record,
> Here ends my strife. If thou invite me forth,
> I rise above abasement at the word.
> Make thy love larger to enlarge my worth.   (NO. 16)

What is the relation between the submissiveness of this poem, and the inequality inherent in patriarchal society? The answer has to be a double one. When Jane Eyre, in a speech which shocked conservative Victorian readers, made her famous declaration of love to Rochester, who was her employer, she did it as an assertion of equality: 'It is my spirit that addresses your spirit; just as if both had passed through the grave, and we stood at God's feet, equal – as we are!' Charlotte Brontë, writing this, was not of course proposing a feminist programme, insisting on a woman's right to vote or to own property: the equality here asserted belongs to the experience of love, and could exist within an unequal society. Similarly, when Elizabeth begins Sonnet 22 with the lines

> When our two souls stand up erect and strong,
> Face to face, silent, drawing nigh and nigher –

this can be read either as shockingly radical or as a commonplace known to everyone (*Jane Eyre* was read both ways by contemporaries). Sonnet 16 seems to be asserting not equality but submission; of course it could be read as an expression of patriarchal inequality, but it could also be a way of telling the 'victor' that the victory is only worthwhile because it is an opportunity to create equality. It is perhaps the simile of the soldier that is most likely to divide the conventional Victorian reading from the modern feminist reading: the conventional reading will have no difficulty in treating the image of warfare as a mere parallel, the feminist may pounce on it as a revelation of the implied violence in gender relationships. And Robert?

The shortest and most famous of Robert's love poems is *Parting at Morning*:

> Round the cape of a sudden came the sea,
> And the sun looked over the mountain's rim;
> And straight was a path of gold for him,
> And the need of a world of men for me.

Conventional as it is, this poem has a strange power: deriving, of course, from the unstated and even mysterious identification between speaker and sun. The sun takes possession of the sea surface so effortlessly and so splendidly that the man immediately and unreflectingly sees it as a role model: 'I want a path of gold too.' *Parting at Morning* follows *Meeting at Night*: it is a counter-aubade. Instead of lamenting the need for lovers to part when their night of love is over (the theme of a hundred medieval aubades), it is spoken by a man who is impatient to be up and doing, and this impatience is offered as part of Nature.

The aubade can, traditionally, be spoken by either man or women, though more often it is given to the woman (even if, as is usually the case, written by a man). There is no countervailing female voice in *Parting at Morning*: Robert Browning's speaker may have spent a happy night with her, but now his only and unqualified wish is to return to the male world. It is exactly in the spirit of Byron's famous line, 'Man's love is of man's life a thing apart; 'Tis woman's whole existence.' A sitting target, this, for the feminist critic, one would think: a resounding statement of the imbalance that feminism sets out to redress. But this, which makes the lines so vulnerable to feminist inversion, is also their strongest defence: they are a simple statement of what is. Byron – and probably Robert Browning too – thought they were stating something inherent in human nature: we think they were describing a social situation, by no means immutable. Since the lines describe not just 19th century Europe but most societies that had up to then existed, their belief is understandable Today we know better – or at least, hope for better.

Robert's most famous poem about gender relations is probably 'A Woman's Last Word':

> Let's contend no more, Love,
> Strive nor weep:
> All be as before, Love,
> – Only sleep!

The technical skill of this poem is remarkable –and prominent: an abab rhyme scheme in stanzas that alternate trimeters with dimeters must call attention to the rhymes, if only because when the lines are so short such a high fraction of the words are rhyme-words. The skill is obviously there to be enjoyed for itself, but no technique can exist wholly in isolation, and its implication is likely to be a confirmation of existing assumptions: why after all would one perform such an elegant metrical dance with existing patterns of thought if one wanted to draw attention to the possibility of rejecting those patterns?

The assumption that is unquestioned is of course that his love renders her submission acceptable:

> Be a god and hold me
> With a charm!
> Be a man and fold me
> With thine arm!

Unquestioned patriarchy: spoken by a woman, in a poem by a man. To read this poem today is, surely, a different experience from a Victorian reading it. We can easily test this, by looking at a Victorian reading:

> In the presence of perfect love words are often superfluous, wild and hurtful; words lead to debate, debate to contention, striving, weeping. Even truth becomes falseness; for if the heart is consecrated by a pure affection, love is the only truth

Not, strictly, Victorian, since Edward Berdoe's *Browning Cyclopaedia* was published in 1912, but it clearly belongs to the world of Robert's original readers. The poem as Berdoe reads it is not quite the poem we read today, for he ignores the feature that is likely to strike us as the most prominent, the sex of the speaker. Berdoe appears to think it is of no importance to the meaning of the poem that a woman is speaking to a man. He tells us that we are in the presence of perfect love; but the lovers have 'contended', and the woman is submitting: a very patriarchal kind of perfect love. In Berdoe's poem, love must be protected against 'words', but he does not appear to have noticed the ambiguity of the term: is the woman saying that silence is appropriate to perfection, so that any words are unnecessary, even damaging? Or did the couple 'have words', is it quarrelling that threatens love? In a society in which devotion and self-sacrifice were constantly presented as feminine virtues, it is hard to imagine the sexes being reversed, and the man weeping a little and submitting.

At what point does a historical shift turn into misreading? A committed reading of a controversial poem (and what poem about gender-relations can fail to be controversial nowadays – or what reader will fail to feel some commitment?) will be an interaction between text and ideology, between what the poem says, and what, for the reader, are the political implications of saying it. The clash that seems to me inevitable between Berdoe's reading and that of the modern reader is partly, I am suggesting, a matter of simple imperceptiveness on his part, but it is partly, also, a historical difference that would arise however perceptive the Victorian reader.

I read the poem as a wonderfully crafted combination of the two ways of viewing the submissive wife – that she is submissive because of the natural superiority of men, and that she is submissive out of pragmatic wisdom, aware that that is the way to handle a husband. Many readers today are aware that women do not have to be constructed in this way, and that most women are no longer willing to be. That is not to misread: it is to situate the same poem in a different frame of possibilities. If we claim – as is probably the case – that the author would have protested against such a reading, then I must point out, politely, that he is not protesting *qua* author, but simply as a Victorian male who does not share our modern frame of possibilities.

The fact that this poem by a man is given a female speaker has not, so far, been a problem: we know that plenty of Victorian women would have shared its assumptions. But it is time we made it a problem: the Victorian woman must be allowed to speak for herself.

> *A Man's Requirements*
> Love me, Sweet, with all thou art,
>   Feeling, thinking, seeing:
> Love me in the lightest part,
>   Love me in full being.
>
> Love me with thine open youth
>   In its frank surrender;
> With the vowing of thy mouth,
>   With its silence tender . . .

Speaking for herself is, of course, not what Elizabeth is here doing, since she too has adopted a persona of the other sex. The man's requirements seem conventionally Victorian, asking for total emotional commitment, implying sexual attraction ('thy blush that burns'), assuming a variety of contrasting moods and situations and hoping to figure in them all – until we come to the final stanza, when the fact that the poem is actually by a woman becomes very important:

> Thus, if thou wilt prove me, Dear,
>   Woman's love no fable,
> I will love thee – half a year –
>   As a man is able.

This changes the whole poem. The blatant cynicism of the conclusion clearly requires us to read the preceding stanzas differently: what had seemed like earnest pleas, to love him in every way possible, now offer themselves light-heartedly, as the airy demands of a man inviting the woman to love him in all the various ways that women, those wonderfully earnest creatures, can manage. What had seemed like delighted acceptance now looks like amusement, to be enjoyed because it is so utterly different from the casual attitude of the male.

Is Elizabeth Browning, then, a cynical poet? That is not the usual picture of her, but we can confirm it in sober prose:

It is true of me – very true – that I have not a high appreciation of what passes in the world . . . under the name of love; and that a distrust of the thing had grown to be a habit of mind with me when I knew you first . . . To see the marriages which are made every day! Worse than solitudes and more desolate! In the case of the two happiest I ever knew, one of the husbands said in confidence to a brother of mine – not much in confidence, or I should not have heard it, but in a sort of smoking frankness, . . . that he had 'ruined his prospects by marrying'; . . . then for the falseness, the first time I ever in my own experience heard that word which rhymes to glove and comes as easily off and on (on some hands!) it was from a man of whose attentions to another woman I was at that time her confidante.

Either of these two husbands would serve as the speaker of 'A Man's Requirements', a poem which regards woman's constancy with a sort of amused admiration, and love as a glove for men to slip on and off.

Of course Elizabeth was not cynical about love, and this letter to Robert is not cynical either, as we can see from the tense of 'had grown to be'. She is showing him the intensity of her present trust by contrasting it with the bitterness from which he has rescued her, allowing herself to say what one isn't supposed to, because of its function as contrast.

Finally, let us look at a poem in which Elizabeth speaks in the voice of a woman, and describes an emotion that may well come from her own experience. Here are the opening stanzas of 'Proof and Disproof', and its ending:

> Dost thou love me, my Belovéd?
>   Who shall answer yes or no?
> What is provéd or disprovéd
>   When my soul inquireth so,
> Dost thou love me, my Belovéd?
>
> I have seen thy heart today,
>   Never open to the crowd,
> While to love me aye and aye
>   Was the vow as it was vowed
> By thine eyes of steadfast grey.

Now I sit alone, alone –
   And the hot tears break and burn,
Now, Belovéd, thou art gone,
   Doubt and terror have their turn,
Is it love that I have known? . . .

Dost thou love me, my Belovéd?
   Only thou canst answer yes!
And, thou gone, the proof's disprovéd,
   And the cry rings answerless –
Dost thou love me, my Belovéd?

I have more than once read this poem with a class of young women, and on each occasion they assumed that it was about an unfaithful, or at least neglectful, man. The situation of a woman in love sitting 'alone, alone', suffering from doubt and terror, asking herself whether he really loves her, was clearly one in which they placed responsibility for her suffering on the man. But I feel certain that this is not how the author intended the poem to be read. Obviously one could bring biographical evidence in here, citing the many letters in which Elizabeth expresses confidence in her husband's love, but I think the poem itself is clear. It is very careful not to tell us anything about the man except that he shows love when he is in her presence: when he is absent, all we are told about is *her* feelings. The point of the title is that the proof is provided by him, the disproof by her: it is a poem about self-doubt.

   And in this case I am reluctant to grant, as I did with 'A Woman's Last Word', that we are faced with two equally possible readings, the latter caused by modern feminist consciousness; here I want to tell my young students that they are mistaken, that they have failed to notice what the poem does (and does not) say, that they have misunderstood the title. But so shadowy is the frontier between a defensible alternative reading and a misreading, that I am not sure I could convince them.

Marian Earle's Fate Worse than Death

It is a truth universally acknowledged that the Victorians treated sex as a taboo subject; yet it is a fact obvious to all readers that the fallen woman appears frequently in their poems and novels. Clearly the taboo consisted not in avoiding the subject, but in certain evasions and restrictions in the manner of treating it. The tension between sympathy and indignation, and that between obeying the rules and striving to be truthful, results in poetic evasiveness but also, in rare moments, in poetic power. This chapter will explore some of those tensions.

We can begin with an actual prostitute. Prostitutes did not write autobiographies, but an accident of history enables us to meet one with refreshing directness:

> Going to the Opera, I met in the Strand one Sarah Tanner, who in 1854 or 5 was a maid of all work to a tradesman in Oxford Street: a lively honest rosy-faced girl, virtuous and self-possessed. A year or so after, I met her in Regent Street arrayed in gorgeous apparel. How is this? said I. Why, she had got tired of service, wanted to see life and be independent; and so she had become a prostitute, of her own accord and without being seduced. She saw no harm in it: enjoyed it very much, thought it might raise her and perhaps be profitable. She had taken it up as a profession, and that with much energy: she had read books, and was taking lessons in writing and other accomplishments, in order to fit herself to be a companion of gentlemen. And her manners were improved – she was no longer vulgar . . . With these advantages and the education she was giving herself, she thought she might get on: for she was not extravagant – she cleaned up her own lodgings, she said, before taking her professional walk.

The eccentric diarist Munby, franker than most men, has preserved this splendidly vivid picture not (one fears) of a typical but certainly of a very real prostitute. For the most part, prostitution was discussed not in such matter of fact but in moral terms, whether the indignation of conventional denunciations, or the compassionate understanding of W. R. Greg, whose article in the *Westminster Review* in 1850 attempted to apply to systematic study of the problem that compassion which sisters of charity did not shrink from applying to individual cases. Indignation and sympathy are very different moral attitudes but they both use moral terminology, in contrast to such a modern scholarly study as Judith Walkowitz's *Prostitution and Victorian Society*, which claims that the 'move into prostitution was in some ways a rational choice, given the limited alternatives open to . . . poor working women'. Sarah Tanner certainly made a rational choice, and she was more successful than most.

And did any Victorian poet manage to shed moralising and show us the world as Sarah Tanner saw it? The conventional treatment, in poems and novels, was very different:

A plunge in the muddy river, a cry on the chill night air,
And the waters upon their bosom a pilgrim sister bear . . .

Touch her not scornfully;
Think of her mournfully . . .

The male poets (here, George R. Sims and Thomas Hood) offer compassion and forgiveness, rather than realism and understanding. One male poet who seems to offer something different is Dante Gabriel Rossetti, whose *Jenny* is the monologue of an ageing roué (not unlike Rossetti himself), who seems to have accompanied Jenny home through kindliness rather than lust:

> Lazy, laughing, languid Jenny,
> Fond of a kiss and fond of a guinea
> Whose head upon my knee tonight
> Rests for a while . . .

As the poem continues, Jenny becomes less laughing, less and less fond of a kiss, and more and more the overworked prostitute, unable to shake off tiredness, but the increase in sympathy goes with an increase in conventionality: the more worthy the attitude, the more predictable the poem.

The one male poet who really could see the world as Sarah Tanner saw it was Thomas Hardy:

> 'O, 'Melia, my dear, this does everything crown!
> Who could have supposed I should meet you in town?
> And whence such fair garments, such prosperi-ty?'
> 'O didn't you know I'd been ruined?' said she.

This ironic ballad is much more closely in touch with folk tradition than the melodrama and pathos of Sims, and in particular with the tradition of the comic ballad spoken by a woman, such as 'The Lass of Islington', in which a vintner tries to renege on his payment for sex, and is brought before a justice with a series of sexual innuendos and made to pay up, ending on a note of delight that the man has been outwitted by a girl who is his social inferior. We don't course know the sex of the author, but the poem must certainly have been enjoyed by generations of working-class girls.

And the female poets? They could, of course, be as conventional as the men: as witness Dora Greenwell, whose 'Christina' is fulsomely pietistic. The speaker in this poem, a repentant prostitute, describes how she was rescued by meeting her childhood friend Christina, who offered 'one drop of love from out of God's great ocean'. In very undistinguished blank verse, the poem uses death for pathos: Christina had lost her infant daughter, and urges the prostitute to be a daughter to her. The speaker, who appears to be dying, concludes by urging the priest to take her cross to Christina.

The sister of the author of 'Jenny' had something of the piety of Greenwell's fictitious Christina; but that did not prevent her writing 'Cousin Kate'. This literary ballad tells about a 'cottage maiden' lured by a 'great lord' to his palace home 'to lead a shameless shameful life', and then discarded so that he can marry her cousin. But this speaker does not repent and die, and the poem ends with a kind of triumph. Cousin Kate was willing to accept soiled goods: if the positions had been reversed, declares the speaker,

> I would have spit into his face
> And not have taken his hand:

(easy, of course, to say that when you have lost the chance); and further, she has a gift Kate 'has not got / And seem[s] not like to get', which is her fair-haired son:

> Your sire would give broad lands for one
> To wear his coronet.

The poem, by the pious and conventional Christina Rossetti, ends less conventionally than it began. It is intended as a comparison between the two women, and the 'great lord' is just there as a prop; but if we are to read it as a poem about sexual politics, how can we not ask about him too? He 'fooled' Kate by wooing her after discarding her cousin: that seems to imply that the same standard of sexual fidelity is expected from him as from a woman. It is hard to know if this is naïve or outspoken. Christina Rossetti, as it happens, had two brothers, who represented two contrasting views of male sexual behaviour: William, the faithful and respectable husband with, as far as we know, only one woman in his life, and Gabriel, whose sexual adventures had little relation to marriage. If Christina regarded William as the norm, then the 'great lord' is doing something unusual in offering his spoilt virtue to Kate: the poem, then, is being naïve. If she regarded Gabriel as the norm, then the poem is being aggressively forthright in claiming that he 'fooled' Kate, since plenty of 19th century husbands, not expecting the same pre-marital chastity of themselves as of women, must have 'fooled' their wives in that way.

As for the last stanza, in which the speaker boasts of her son, it can be regarded as a claim that Nature does not underwrite conventional morality: the respectable wife is not rewarded with motherhood, the cast-off mistress is. The same situation occurs in George Eliot's *Silas Marner*. It is a kind of confirmation of Edmund's salute to bastards in *King Lear*, with its contrast between 'the lusty stealth of nature' and the 'dull, stale, tired bed' of matrimony.

But there are two sustained and powerful versions of the fallen woman in 19th century poetry, to which I now turn. Both are by women.

Stealing, Murder, Female Bonding

First, there is Marian Erle, whose story occupies the second half of Elizabeth Browning's 'novel in verse'. Marian emerged from a childhood of poverty and temptation with her virginity intact: in fact it was to preserve her virtue (to escape, in the Victorian cliché, a fate worse than death) that she ran away from home and so was condemned to even worse poverty. Her mother thrust her into confronting a man 'with beast's eyes and burning stertorous breath' whom she refers to as 'the squire', declaring 'he means to set you up and comfort us'; Marian fled to shelter in a ditch, followed by fever, hospital, and rescue by Romney Leigh. Her virtue having been established in this melodramatic fashion, it is naturally a shock for Aurora, meeting her in Paris, to find she has become an unmarried mother. The ensuing encounter is one of the most interesting moments in all Victorian poetry.

How much did Elizabeth Browning know about the world she was depicting? Deirdre David has pointed out that her literary practice was 'almost exclusively textual'. She led a secluded and very literary life, was an invalid until her marriage, and wrote what were often literary and allusive poems. Almost certainly she never met a prostitute: does that matter? Should poets or novelists write about what they know?

Charles Dickens must have had a first-hand knowledge of fallen women unrivalled among Victorian writers. He was virtually the director of Urania Cottage, the home for rehabilitating prostitutes financed by Angela Burdett Coutts: he was shrewd and knowledgeable in drawing up its regulations, and in handling awkward cases. Yet his portrayal of female sexuality and of fallen women is completely conventional – far more so than the 'textual' knowledge of Elizabeth Browning. First-hand knowledge is no guarantee of freedom from convention.

To appreciate the power of the encounter between Aurora and Marian, it will be best to move through the story in the order in which it happens, not in the order of narration. In Paris, Marian was raped; after the initial trauma was over, she found a situation as a lady's maid with a 'young and light' mistress, who

> Was easy with me, less for kindness than
> Because she led, herself, an easy time
> Betwixt her lover and her looking glass . . .   (VII, 22)

When this easy-going mistress discovered (before Marian herself!) that her maid was pregnant, she dismissed her without compunction and with a virtuously indignant speech:

> 'Twas natural of course
> She should not ask me where I meant to sleep;
> I might sleep well beneath the heavy Seine,
> Like others of my sort . . .
> I broke on Marian there. 'Yet she herself
> A wife, I think, had scandals of her own,
> A lover not her husband.'
> 'Ay,' she said,
> But gold and meal are measured otherwise;
> I learned so much at school,' said Marian Erle.   (VII, 78)

Ideologically, as well as poetically, a great deal is going on here. Blame for the suicide of the fallen woman is given in class terms; there is an explicit, indignant condemnation of the mistress, and that is (shrewdly) attributed to the respectable Aurora, who can afford to be surprised at such callousness. Marian, in contrast, accepts it with a cynical working-class shrug, in that last, unpoetic line, one of the most powerful in her narrative. If she learned it at school, it would, of course, have been from her fellow pupils, since it was certainly not on the syllabus!

Those are the strengths of the passage; but it has two weaknesses. First, Marian's surprise when she is told she is pregnant (after eight months!): such ignorance seems unlikely in any woman, however sheltered her upbringing, and doubly unlikely in the hard-headed working-class girl who had so clearly learnt the facts of life at school (sexual facts, surely, as well as economic). It is, of course, a ploy by the author to increase our sympathy for the victim, and it protests too much. And second, the blatant hypocrisy of the mistress weakens the social analysis. Hypocrisy, always an easy target, detracts from ideological conflict: the claim that the rich do not really believe their own moral code is a way of selecting the easiest targets for satire. The real conflicts are those in which two genuine ideals clash, and this is what we find in Book six.

Aurora meets Marian in Paris by accident: a strained coincidence, but it produces some haunting images as she glimpses, for a moment, a once-known face in the crowd. When eventually she tracks Marian down, learns that she has a child, and reproaches her for it, the encounter is charged with emotion: distress, blame, anger. Most interesting, in this 'textual' poet, is the vocabulary in which it is conducted.

Now that the basic Anglo-Saxon terms have lost their taboo, the vocabulary of sex has been transformed to a point that would leave a Victorian baffled; to appreciate what is being said, and not said, between Marian and Aurora, we need to hear their conversation with Victorian ears. Bluntness was impossible; but, to the evasiveness that convention demanded, each of the women adds a further (and revealing) evasiveness of her own. 'Illegitimate' or 'born out of wedlock' are perfectly accept-able terms for a respectable woman to use in 1861, but Aurora does not use them: her word is 'stealing'.

> 'The priest who stole a lamb to offer him,
> Was still a thief. And if a woman steals
> (Through God's own barrier hedges of true love,
> Which fence out licence in securing love)
> A child like this, that smiles so in her face,
> She is no mother but a kidnapper . . .   (VI, 632)

'Rape' is almost equally acceptable as a term, but Marian does not use it:

> I was not ever, as you say, seduced,
> But simply, murdered.   (VI, 770)

These are not euphemisms but, if anything, the opposite: both women choose terms that make the transgression sound more, not less, extreme. To think of illegitimate sex as theft is to regard sexual activity as prop-erty, that must only be used by the rightful owner. Only children born in wedlock can be said to belong to the mother, and unlicensed sex is seen as climbing over fences established by God, in order to steal what does not belong to you. Now thieves do not break in because they enjoy climbing fences, but because they want the loot – in this case, the child: women, in this version of unlicensed sex, are in search not of sexual pleasure but of motherhood. If we turn back to the encounter with 'the squire' in Book three, we can see that there too the possibility of sex as a source of pleasure or as entry into womanhood is not even considered. Sexual initiation, for a woman, is physically loathsome, an entry only into degradation or motherhood.

Such is the evasiveness of Aurora's term, 'stealing'. Marian's evasiveness is different, deriving from the familiar cliché of the fate worse then death: a kind of ruthless logic leads from the cliché to the term 'murder' for rape. 'I was not ever, as you say, seduced': the thought that she might have consented is so repulsive to Marian that she will only admit the term 'seduced' into her vocabulary by making it clear that it is Aurora's word, not hers. As for 'simply', it has a double function: first, it declares that there was no trace of consent from her, it was a simple act of violence, and second, it insists that 'murder' – like 'fate worse than death' – is hardly a metaphor, that being raped is just the same as being killed.

Marian insists on the term 'murdered' at obsessive length:

> I'm dead, I say,
> And if, to save the child from death as well,
> The mother in me has survived the rest,
> Why, that's God's miracle you must not tax,
> I'm not less dead for that: I'm nothing more
> But just a mother.   (VI, 821)

If we put aside the insistence on miracle, we can see the truth of this: that as a single mother she has lost all opportunity to live as an individual, and is reduced to one function only.

But it is not only for its vocabulary that this encounter is so significant. If we turn from the language to the substance of what they say, we can perceive a clash between two great Victorian ideals: sanctity of marriage, and sanctity of motherhood. Illegitimacy is disturbing precisely because it can put these two ideals into conflict:

> I have as sure a right
> As any glad proud mother in the world,
> Who sets her darling down to cut his teeth
> Upon her church-ring. If she talks of law,
> I talk of law! I claim my mother-dues

By law – the law which now is paramount –
The common law, by which the poor and weak
Are trodden underfoot by vicious men,
And loathed for ever after by the good.   (VI, 661)

There are plenty of hard objects for a child to cut its teeth on: Marian chooses to mention the wedding ring in order to say that legitimacy is trivial compared with caring. The splendid defiance of these lines then turns Aurora's image of 'stealing' back against her, as Marian claims the 'dues' to which motherhood entitles her. The parallel with law is used with great precision: Aurora appealed to the official moral rules, which can be likened to statute law, and Marian responds by appealing to 'common law', which is of course a pun: on the one hand it means the practice of abusing poor women, which is so common (as when we say 'jungle law'), but on the other it means 'case law', built up from precedents, and so based on actual experience, not statutes.

Then Marian goes even further: she wishes that Aurora had never come 'to make me sob until I vex the child': morality can actually interfere with mothering, and must be brushed aside. This splendid turning of one Victorian ideal against another is so powerful that it is a disappointment to learn that Marian was the innocent victim of rape, that she is not a sexual rebel but a passive victim. We had not yet been told this: that is why this discussion began from the order of events, since the order of narration is a kind of trick, describing the motherhood *before* mention of the rape. One anticipation of modern ideas now subsides into convention – but is immediately replaced by another, in this poem which is so full of anticipations: Aurora proposes that they should live together and bring up the child:

> . . . henceforth thou and I
> Being still together will not miss a friend,
> Nor he a father, since two mothers shall
> Make that up to him.   (VII, 122)

The idea of two women forming a parental unit, and rendering the father unnecessary, is today associated with lesbianism, since we now assume that sexual activity is the wish and right of everyone; here of course it is assumed that the two women living together will make sex unnecessary – so much so that the female 'marriage' must be presented not in sexual but in religious imagery:

And in my Tuscan home I'll find a niche
And set thee there, my saint, the child and thee,
And burn the lights of love before thy face,
And ever at thy sweet look cross myself
From mixing with the world's prosperities.   (VII, 126)

Now we are in a convent: the setting is not bedroom but chapel. But convents, after all, are also a form of female bonding.

The last two books of *Aurora Leigh* are, as I believe and as is widely thought, the least successful, as so much of its subversive potential is retracted in order to make a happy ending – as so often happens in Victorian novels, where the conventional world is challenged but is reaffirmed in the end by the nervous novelist, who finds it necessary to make the shrewd radical character repent, thus leaving bourgeois readers comfortable And the nervousness of the bourgeois novelists about subverting class assumptions can be paralleled to Elizabeth Browning's nervousness about subverting gender assumptions.

And should we blame them for this? They believed that conflict could and should be subsumed in reconciliation, and subsequent history has shown that in the long run they were probably correct. But literary works do not exist only in the long run; and readers who respond to the explosive brilliance of the subversive elements, in novel or in poem, can be forgiven for regretting the way all comes right. Millamant, at the end of *The Way of the World*, is going to surrender her female independence and live happily ever after with Mirabel; but who can resist the sigh with which she concedes that she 'may, by degrees, dwindle into a wife'. Aurora no doubt will also live happily ever after; but she has dwindled.

A Castaway

Finally, Augusta Webster: less famous than Elizabeth Browning, perhaps not so fine a poet, but with a shrewdness unequalled by anyone else when it came to treating the fallen woman.

A Castaway is a monologue spoken by a courtesan who has made a success of her life It moves easily between conventional features – reminiscences of her ordinary, virtuous and dull girlhood, the death of her infant son – and a good deal of Sarah Tanner realism. The more or less predictable episodes – alienation from her respectable brother, parting from the father of her dead child – are told with some startling touches of realism: in both cases, she refused the money they tried to give her, and in both cases she is not at all sure she was right:

Money's the root of evil do they say?
Money is virtue, strength: money to me
Would then have been repentance: could I live
Upon my idiot's pride?   (594)

That 'money' was the lover's money: in the case of her brother she
begged for help and then sent the money back: 'that's like me too.'

Webster's realism both exposes the dreariness of the virtuous alterna-
tives, and shows the complexities of the life the speaker chose. There is
therefore a striking account of the dreariness of governessing that sounds
like one of Charlotte Brontë's letters versified:

. . . plod and plod and drum the sounds
Of useless facts into unwilling ears,
Tease children with dull questions half the day
Then con dull answers in my room at night
Ready for next day's questions, mend quill pens
And cut my fingers, add up sums done wrong
And never get them right; teach, teach and teach . . .
                                                (335)

– and on the other hand a shorter but equally startling account of
conventional wifehood, brilliantly embodied in a single piece of word-
play, in the description of the brother's wife:

A dapper little madam dimple cheeked
And dimple brained, who makes him a good wife.   (610)

As she reflects on the bleak outlook of her own future, it is not guilt
and repentance which dominate, but the fear of growing old:

How one would clutch at youth to hold it tight!
And then to know it gone, to see it gone,
Be taught its absence by harsh careless looks,
To live forgotten, solitary, old –
The cruellest word that ever woman learns.   (175)

There are several moments of striking verbal awareness in the poem,
including an ability to build on the prohibitions of the language. Perhaps
the most brilliant passage occurs near the beginning: looking in the
mirror, she feels herself a woman still, 'With still some little pride, some

little —', then pulls herself up as she realises that the word she wants is 'modesty':

> A wanton I, but modest! Modest, true;
> I'm not drunk in the streets, ply not for hire
> At infamous corners with my likenesses
> Of the humblest kind; yes, modesty's my word —
> 'Twould shape my mouth well too, I think I'll try:
> 'Sir, Mr What-you-will, Lord Who-knows-what,
> My present lover or my next to come,
> Value me at my worth, fill your purse full,
> For I am modest;
>
> But she isn't: she is
>   that thing
> Called half a dozen dainty names, and none
> Dainty enough to serve the turn and hide
> The one coarse English word that lurks beneath:
> Just that, no worse, no better.   (46)

In the unrestraint of Elizabethan English a play could be called 'The Honest Whore'; but the comparable oxymoron 'modest whore' must, in Victorian English, remain unspoken. Yet its truth is manifest: because she is so successful a whore, she can treat herself to modesty, and because there is no inhibition attached to that word she can toy with it in a kind of bitter amusement: what remains unspoken is the irony attaching to it, for irony always consists in leaving something unspoken. 'Whore', on the other hand, is a word unbecoming to modest lips, so the poem does not utter it, and the evasiveness makes us aware that there are two quite different reasons for the avoidance: the Bowdlerian reason, that respectable discourse (including the poem) must not use words that would bring a blush to a maiden's cheek, and the very different reason that so successful a prostitute has earned ('earned') the right not to be described so bluntly.

How did the blameless Mrs Webster know all this? She could not claim special insight simply on the basis of being female, but she was active in both journalism and campaigning for women's rights. Whatever the reason, she conveys a truer knowledge of sexual politics than do virtually any of her male contemporaries. This can lead us to wonder whether, among Victorians, a man or a woman was more likely to know how a woman in that situation felt — the man because he or his friends may have been a customer, or the woman because her dealings with brothers, father and husband will have given her experiences that have something in common with being a castaway.

Note *Aurora Leigh* can of course be found in Elizabeth Browning's poems, and there are two good modern editions: in the World's Classics, edited with a good introduction by Kerry McSweeney; and with a great deal of contemporary material and modern criticism in the Norton Critical Edition, edited by Margaret Reynolds. Munby's encounter with Sarah Tanner can be found in Derek Hudson, *Munby: Man of Two Worlds* (London, 1974). W. R. Greg's article on Prostitution appeared in the *Westminster Review,* no. 53 (1850), and is reprinted in the Norton Critical Edition. Hardy's ironic ballad is called 'The Ruined Maid'. 'The Lass of Islington can be found in *The Popular Muse*, edited by Rodway and de Sola Pinto (London, 1957). Deirdre David's discussion of the poem, cited in this chapter, is in *Intellectual Women and Victorian Patriarchy* (London, 1987). *A Castaway* is in *Victorian Women Poets*, edited by Leighton and Reynolds; and Augusta Webster is further discussed in 'Three Radicals', later in this book.

Emily Brontë

Two contexts call out for Emily Brontë's poetry, one her own, the other very public: both, perhaps, need to be resisted. The first is Gondal, the second is Christianity.

The Brontës have, of course, become an industry. Their home at Haworth attracts thousands of visitors (one dare not speculate how many have actually read their works), their saucepans are viewed by tourists who (perhaps) mingle reverence with relief that we don't use such things today, and their private lives and secretive writings are edited and expounded by scholars. 'Scholars', in this context, includes many whose interest might be described as the higher gossip: uncovering not only the details of their lives, but also the personal stories they devoted long hours to, and kept secret. Charlotte and Branwell made up stories about a West African kingdom called Angria, inhabited by figures from a romanticised military history, and the youngest sisters, Emily and Anne, invented the kingdom of Gondal, vaguely situated in the Pacific ocean, inhabited by a large cast of romantic figures enacting tales of love and death. Far more material about Gondal than about Angria has survived, including poems composed by and addressed to Rosina Alcona, her lovers, and a large cast of invented figures. For a certain kind of scholar, this offers an irresistible temptation, and there have been meticulous attempts to reconstruct the whole Gondal story from the tiny notebooks they left, and to place the poems into it. Here is the opening of one of her most famous poems:

> Cold in the earth, and the deep snow piled above thee!
> Far, far removed, cold in the dreary grave!
> Have I forgot, my only love, to love thee,
> Severed at last by Time's all-wearing wave?

Some anthologies simply call this 'The Prisoner', others entitle it 'R. Alcona to J. Brenzaida' . These are of course two figures from the Gondal stories, and if we set out to find who they are we would find ourselves on a long journey of research among documents that were never intended to be read by strangers. When Charlotte persuaded her sister to let her poems appear in their joint publication, this poem lost the one trace of its origin in the Gondal story: whereas the dead figure had been buried on 'Angora's shore', this was now changed to 'that northern shore'. Clearly the sisters' own publication was willing to rescue the poem from the private context to which Brontë scholars are keen to return it.

It is even arguable that removing the Gondal context makes the poems not only more accessible but better. 'The Prisoner' is the best example of this. It opens melodramatically:

> In the dungeon crypts idly did I stray,
> Reckless of the lives wasting there away;
> 'Draw the ponderous bars! Open, Warder stern!'
> He dared not say me nay – the hinges harshly turn

It is hard to imagine a worse stanza than this: why should someone wandering through dungeons do so 'idly', then suddenly command the warder so stagily to open the bars, and then be obeyed so promptly? The narrator then meets a female prisoner, who is taunted by the warder and declares that

> A messenger of Hope comes every night to me,
> And offers for short life, eternal liberty.

'Then dawns the invisible', and at that point the poem suddenly becomes intensely compelling, as a vision of freedom is given and then snatched away:

Oh! dreadful is the check – intense the agony –
When the ear begins to hear, and the eye begins to see:
When the pulse begins to throb, the brain to think again;
The soul to feel the flesh, and the flesh to feel the chain.

The agony of returning from vision to life again is a central theme of
visionary writing, and the poem seems to have dropped its narrative and
now concentrates on the painful intensity of the return to consciousness.
The last word of this stanza may of course refer to the actual chain binding
the prisoner, or to the body, imagined as a chain on the soul that had felt
itself escaping. Andrew Marvell's *Dialogue between the Soul and the Body*,
written two hundred years before this poem, also imagined the soul as
enchained in the body:

> A soul hung up, as 'twere, in chains
> Of nerves and arteries and veins.

Marvell's metaphysical wit makes it clear that the soul feels itself a pris-
oner simply because it is in the body, so that 'chains' is purely a metaphor
here. Emily Brontë does not delight in wit as the seventeenth century
poet does, and the fact that the body in her poem is really in chains may
do more harm than good to her poem here. She may well have felt herself
that the mystical experience of being taken away from and then returned
to the body was what this poem is really about; certainly all the editors
and anthologists who have removed the melodramatic narrative setting
leaving only the painful experience of being taken out of the body and
having to return to it, have felt something like that.

Probably no poem by Emily Brontë removes all explanatory setting
more completely that this short one:

> The night is darkening round me,
> The wild winds coldly blow,
> But a tyrant spell has bound me
> And I cannot, cannot go.
>
> The giant trees are bending,
> Their bare boughs weighed with snow
> And the storm is fast descending
> And yet I cannot go.

Cloud beyond clouds above me,
Wastes beyond wastes below,
But nothing drear can move me
I will not, cannot go.

Nothing is here explained. Who is the tyrant? Where does she wish to go – forward or backwards: further into the snowstorm, to some longed-for goal, or out of it, back into shelter? It looks as if the poem itself has been frozen, refusing to tell us any of these things. We can believe, if it helps, that there is a story behind the poem, and that the Gondal materials will explain it (though they don't); but the story is known only to the poet (and perhaps to Anne), and in an important sense the poem has been extracted from it – and it owes its strange power to this.

So much for Gondal. The Brontë girls were the daughters of a parson, and naturally grew up in an atmosphere of conventional Christian belief; Charlotte, after reading Harriet Martineau's *Letters on the Nature & Development of Man* ('the first exposition of avowed atheism and materialism I have ever read') was appalled: 'If this be the Truth, man or woman who beholds her can but curse the day he or she was born.' Anne wrote some very conventionally Christian poems, in which 'A sinless God for sinful men Descends to suffer and to bleed.' And Emily?

No coward soul is mine
No trembler in the world's storm-troubled sphere.
I see Heaven's glory shine
And Faith shines equal arming me from Fear.

O God within my breast
Almighty ever present Deity
Life that in me hast rest
As I Undying Life, have power in thee.

The pious reader might well read these lines untroubled, taking 'faith' to mean Christian faith and the Deity invoked to be the Christian God; and some such trust may well be responsible for this becoming (probably) Emily's most loved poem; but the next stanza could give us pause:

Vain are the thousand creeds
That move men's hearts, unutterably vain,

Worthless as withered weeds
Or idlest froth amid the boundless main.

Are these *other* creeds, as any Christian might maintain; or are we being told that all creeds are vain, that the God within her breast cannot be fitted into *any* theology? Certainly the lines do not feel like Christian apologetics: the dismissive sweep of 'Vain are the thousand creeds' hardly suggests it will be followed by 'Except for ours' ; it feels more like a dismissal of theology as mere formulae, an insistence that words cannot spell out the meaning.

The pious reader who does not scrutinise her poems is not likely to feel distressed; but readers today are less pious, and perhaps more inclined to scrutinise. So what do we now make of her poem addressed to *The Night wind,* which 'told me Heaven was glorious / And sleeping Earth was fair', and which she resists, telling it to

Play with the scented flower,
The young tree's supple bough –
And leave my human feelings
In their own course to flow.

The wind is given the last word: they have been friends and will be so until she lies in the churchyard: then

I shall have time enough to mourn
And thou to be alone.

This haunting poem has some kind of argument, but what is it? Is the wind trying to woo her into a kind of pantheism and away from her Christian faith – and is it succeeding? It could even be the other way round. Poem after poem of Emily Brontë's seems to address questions of belief, but never quite to engage with them: there is an argument going on, but what is being maintained?

A curious parallel here is with the treatment of love in *Wuthering Heights*. Everyone who praises this novel treats it as a great and powerful love story, but it contains no love scene. What are the famous passages about the intense love between Catherine and Heathcliff? There is Catherine's famous declaration to Nelly that her love for him is 'like the eternal rocks', which she makes when Heathcliff is not present; there are passionate scenes after she has married Linton, which consist almost entirely of rebukes ('Why shouldn't you suffer? I do!'); and there are elaborate accounts of Heathcliff's intense grief after she is dead. The only love *scene* in the novel is between Hareton and the younger Cathy towards the end. It is as if love, like God, is something Brontë could not talk about head-on.

There is of course a further question we can put to her poems: not only whether they should be detached from Gondal, or from Christianity, but also how good they are. And this is just as tantalising as the others. True, such a question is always tantalising, since the excellence or bad-ness of poetry is not something that can be demonstrated with even the assurance with which meaning can be explored, but this often seems even more true of these Brontë poems because of the narrow line between the successful and the trite.

> *Stars*
> Ah! why, because the dazzling sun
> Restored our Earth to joy,
> Have you departed, every one,
> And left a desert sky?

Not, surely, a promising opening to what Robin Grove, in an interesting essay, suggests may be her best poem; and the poem does turn out to be a haunting suggestion that the stars bring peace and the sun is a kind of bully:

> Blood-red he rose, and, arrow-straight,
> His fierce beams struck my brow;
> The soul of nature sprang, elate,
> But *mine* sank sad and low!

– I could do without the overinsistent italics (plus exclamation mark!) in the last line, but the suggestion that the (usually life-giving) sun is a kind of bully gives the poem an interestingly personal touch:

> My lids closed down, yet through their veil
> I saw him blazing, still,
> And steep in gold the misty dale,
> And flash upon the hill.

The last two lines could easily belong in a poem of eager praise of the life-giving sunrise, and the reversal of the usual response makes this a fascinatingly personal poem:

Oh, stars, and dreams, and gentle night:
Oh, night and stars, return!
And hide me from the hostile light
That does not warm, but burn.

We can amuse ourselves speculating that the bullying sun here represents Reason, or God, or the Reverend Patrick Brontë, or simply what is expected in a poem, or all of these and more. Certainly it represents the expected, and makes the poem interestingly eccentric. The expected that turns out to be more eccentric than we at first realised – that seems to be the recipe for a poem by Emily Brontë

Note   There are several editions of Emily Brontë's poems, including that edited by Barbara Lloyd-Evans (London, 1992) and the *Complete Poems* edited by C. W. Hatfield (London, 1941). *The Art of Emily Brontë*, edited by Anne Smith (London, 1976) contains two good essays on her poetry, by Barbara Hardy and by Robin Grove.

Prepare your Fortitude: George Eliot

In March 1867 George Eliot wrote to tell her publisher, John Blackwood, that the work she had been writing 'is not a Romance. It is – prepare your fortitude – a poem.' That his best-selling novelist should send him a long poem is not, perhaps, good news for any publisher (though Blackwood took it well, and liked the poem – or said he did). Is it surprising that our greatest woman novelist, perhaps our greatest novelist, should have had ambitions as a poet? Yes, if we think of the solidities of fiction, its engagement with social reality, as a contrast to the ethereal beauties of poetry. No, if we think of both fiction and poetry as explorations of how experience can translate into language – language (as Pound's famous definition of poetry has it) 'charged with meaning to the highest possible degree'.

The poem which George Eliot imposed on Blackwood's fortitude was *The Spanish Gypsy*, a story of passion, honour and religious zeal set in Spain at the end of the 15th century. She chose the title 'because it is a little in the fashion of the elder dramatists, with whom I have perhaps more cousinship than with recent poets'. She was quite right in claiming, when she wrote verse, 'cousinship' with the elder dramatists, as we can see from the verse epigraphs to some of the chapters in *Middlemarch*. When no source is given for these passages they were (we presume) by

George Eliot herself, and many of them are not only 'in the fashion of the elder dramatists' but among her finest bits of verse – sometimes pithily sententious:

> Our deeds still travel with us from afar,
> And what we have been makes us what we are

(her summary of how Bulstrode's past catches up on him in chapter 70) – and sometimes with a kind of metaphysical wit:

> Nay, power is relative; you cannot fright
> The coming pest with border fortresses,
> Or catch your carp with subtle argument.
> All force is twain in one: cause is not cause
> Unless effect be there; and action's self
> Must needs contain a passive

(which introduces Lydgate's failure to win the battle of wills with his wife.) They often sound like a fine moment in a long poem –

> Surely the golden hours are turning grey
> And dance no more, and vainly strive to run;
> I see their white locks streaming in the wind –
> Each face is haggard as it looks at me,
> Slow-turning in the constant clasping round
> Storm-driven –

The 'haggard face' that looks out of these lines is of course a metaphor (it belongs to the hours) but is also powerfully and suggestively literal: in some disturbing way a human as well as a metaphorical face – perhaps even, for a frightening instant, the face of the dead Casaubon. The lines seems to describe both the way the dying Casaubon sees the world and also, mysteriously, the way that the world itself now appears – to the author? to Dorothea? to you and me? There are few moments as powerful as these in *The Spanish Gypsy*: George Eliot, when writing verse, has stamina, of a rather pedestrian kind, but real genius only in moments.

By writing in verse, and by setting her long poem in the 15th century, George Eliot removed it doubly from the bracing realism of her modern novels. Her historical novel *Romola,* set, as it happens, at much the same time, though in Italy, not in Spain, is only once removed; this enables us

to ask which is more important to her realism, the use of prose or the
modern setting. One generalising sentence in *Romola* tells us that her trust

> had been delusive, but she would have chosen over again to have acted
> on it rather than be a creature led by phantoms and disjointed whispers
> in a world where there was the large music of reasonable speech, and the
> warm grasp of living hands.

Few sentences sum up George Eliot's view of life as well as this one.
Though it is from a historical novel, it bears no trace of the 15th century
Florence that she recreated so carefully: prose enables it to emerge from
the 15th century, but apart from that one can see that a generalisation
like this really needs prose, in order to give its point the appropriate
sobriety.

But *The Spanish Gypsy*, though her most ambitious poem, is not her
most successful; almost all of her shorter poems offer as much and are
much less daunting. *The Legend of Jubal* shows how close she could come
to Keats

> – feel the sweet unrest
> Of the world's spring-tide in thy conscious breast –

and *Armgart* explores a situation that could figure in one of her novels,
that of the singer who gives up everything (and forces others to give up
much) for her art, and then finds she has lost her voice. We begin by
seeing Armgart at the height of her powers:

> – Pouring her passion on the air made live
> With human heart-throbs. Tell them, Leo, tell them
> How I outsang your hope and made you cry
> Because Gluck could not hear me –

And then, when mistaken medical help destroys her voice, we see her
refusing the anodyne that would

> Drug me to sleep that I may wake again
> Without a purpose, abject as the rest
> To bear the yoke of life.

It would be unlike George Eliot to end on a purely negative note, so
Armgart is given a kind of acceptance of her lot when she decides to teach

music and live with her crippled cousin Walpurga who had sacrificed her own life for Armgart. A moral ending: but less powerful than the speech in which Walpurga tells her that her earlier success had been selfish, and that her single-minded pursuit of her career was elitist:

> Ay, such a mask
> As the few born like you to easy joy,
> Cradled in privilege, take for natural
> On all the lowly faces that must look
> Upward to you!

(Women who become great singers need – and 'take for natural' – the support of the Walpurgas: which can be seen as saying that feminism is elitist).

And since I suggested that the theme of *Armgart* could figure in one of her novels, I should have added that it did. The prose version of Armgart is Al-Charisi, the singer who appears at the end of *Daniel Deronda*. She too lost her voice and lost a great career, but with the extra irony that after she had irrevocably given up her career she regained her voice:

> I made believe that I preferred being the wife of a Russian noble to being the greatest lyric actress of Europe; I made believe – I acted that part. It was because I felt my greatness sinking away from me . . . I would not wait till men said, 'She had better go.'

Al-Charisi appears in only two chapters of the seventy in *Daniel Deronda*, but her effect on the novel is shattering: she articulates all the resistance which readers may have been feeling to the message of the book, and her own story is as powerful as two chapters make possible. There is nothing as powerful, as succinct, and as bitter as this in *Armgart*.

Most widely read among her poems is the set of eleven sonnets called *Brother & Sister*, because they use the same material as *The Mill on the Floss*; and once again the advantages of prose over verse are clear.

> Long years have left their writing on my brow,
> But yet the freshness and the dew-fed beam
> Of those young mornings are about me now . . .

We learn to restrain ourselves as we get older. We keep apart when we have quarrelled, express ourselves in well-bred phrases, and in this way preserve a dignified alienation showing much firmness on one side, and swallowing much grief on the other.

It would be rash to claim that sober reflections on how childhood differs from adulthood need always be in prose, but when they are by George Eliot they clearly do. The temptation to coin phrasing like 'dew-fed beam' is too strong when she writes verse, and she loses the succinct generalisation of that first sentence, and the slight hint of personal experience behind the ending of the sentence. She is a natural prose-writer, and not a natural poet.

So does George Eliot's poetry owe its interest entirely to its being by the author of her novels? That seems to be the lurking conclusion, but I wish to end on a more positive note – and also, perhaps, a quite unexpected one. Two of George Eliot's poems, both in blank verse, have received little attention and less praise: 'A College Breakfast Party', in which a set of dons with names out of *Hamlet* indulge in some very abstruse philosophising, and 'A Minor Prophet', which describes the Utopian views of the poet's friend,

> a vegetarian seer,
> By name Elias Baptist Butterworth,
> A harmless, bland, disinterested man.

These two pedestrian poems drift, at times, into a kind of quaint profundity. 'A Minor Prophet' makes fun of Butterworth's Utopianism, pitying the men

> Who living in those perfect future times
> Will not know half the dear imperfect things
> That move my smiles and tears,

but its rendering of Utopianism has a quaint charm, and after making fun of the perfectionists it concludes with an oddly profound celebration of their 'presentiment of better things on earth', which

> Sweeps like the sense of vastness, when at night
> We hear the roll and dash of waves that break
> Nearer and nearer with the rushing tide,
> Which rises to the level of the cliff
> Because the wide Atlantic rolls behind
> Throbbing respondent to the far-off orbs.

'A College Breakfast Party' is even odder, and at times very obscure. But when it toys with a quite irreligious way of finding meaning in the universe, it can, surprisingly, sound like Wallace Stevens:

> The universe, I hold, is no charade,
> No acted pun unriddled by a word,
> Nor pain a decimal diminishing
> With hocus-pocus of a dot or nought.
> For those who know it, pain is solely pain . . .

This is not the only moment at which her lines, unexpectedly, remind us of Stevens, and not only because of the intrusive – and Stevens-like – 'I hold'. She like him has heard the vanity

> Which finds the universe beneath its mark,
> And scorning the blue heavens as merely blue
> Can only say, 'What then'.

He, like her, watches as

> the sea
> And heaven rolled as one and from the two
> Came fresh transfigurings of freshest blue.

The man with the blue guitar has, for a moment, been anticipated by a woman who couples a colour with an abstraction as Stevens was so brilliantly to do. The great 19th century agnostic strikes an echo from the great agnostic of the 20th century.

Christina Rossetti

> Morning and evening
> Maids hear the goblins cry:
> Apples and quinces,
> Lemons and oranges,
> Plump unpecked cherries,
> Melons and raspberries,
> Bloom-down-cheeked peaches,
> Swart-headed mulberries,
> Wild free-born cranberries,
> Crab-apples, dewberries,
> Pine-apples, blackberries,

> Apricots, strawberries; –
> All ripe together
> In summer weather . . .
> Come buy, come buy.'

'All ripe together' indeed! They must be magic fruits: if we read atten-
tively, we can know even before the story begins (for this is the
opening of the poem) that there is something unnatural about these
fruits.

Lizzie and Laura are two sisters who live affectionately together
(without, evidently, any other family); Lizzie insists that they should not
'peep at goblin men', or buy their fruits – 'Who knows upon what soil
they fed / Their hungry, thirsty roots' – but Laura is tempted, thinking

> How fair the vine must grow
> Whose grapes are so luscious;
> How warm the wind must blow
> Thro' those fruit bushes.

So Laura goes to meet the goblins, and since she has no money the
goblins take one of her golden curls, and she eats the fruit. When she
rejoins her sister, she finds she can no longer hear the goblin men. 'Laura
turned as cold as stone / To find her sister heard that cry alone', and she
begins to waste away. Lizzie rescues her by taking a golden penny and
going to meet the goblins, refusing to taste the fruit, but allowing them
to smear the juices all over her. This annoys the goblins so much that
they fling back her penny, and Lizzie runs home, crying out to Laura

> Hug me, kiss me, suck my juices
> Squeezed from goblin fruits for you,
> Eat me, drink me, love me;
> Laura, make much of me:
> For your sake I have braved the glen
> And had to do with goblin merchant men.

Laura does just that, and is cured. The poem ends with a glimpse of the
two girls grown-up and with children of their own, and with a simple
moral reflection: 'There is no friend like a sister.'

Goblin Market is Christina Rossetti's most celebrated and, by common
consent, her finest poem. How do we interpret its strange story? Rossetti
declared that the poem had no symbolic significance, insisting that 'she

did not mean anything profound', and the only conclusion explicitly offered is the rather trite remark that 'there is no friend like a sister'; but no sophisticated modern reader – and perhaps not many unsophisticated ones – can refrain from asking what the fruits symbolise. Rossetti's disclaimer may simply mean that interpreters are saved the trouble of admitting that their interpretation differs from the author's, since the author offered none.

The obvious interpretation is that the fruits stand for sex; and the mention of Jeanie, who 'for joys brides hope to have Fell sick and died', seems to confirm this. Jeanie ate the goblin fruits, 'dwindled and grew grey', and now 'no grass will grow' on her grave. This episode is so like the moral warning provided by the familiar Victorian picture of the fallen woman that it naturally suggests a sexual reading of the story: indeed fits such a reading much better than anything we are told about Laura herself. The conclusion, that shows us the two sisters grown up and married with children of their own, clearly shows that on one level at least the goblins' fruits do not represent sex (though we can always point out that Lizzie and Laura have children but no mention of husbands). Critics have offered interpretations ('women's common plight as commodities in the linked capitalist and sexual economies') that seem to describe their own interests more than Rossetti's – as critics often do. What seems to me the most consistent interpretation (but not one I have seen proposed) would say that it's about homeopathy, since Laura is cured by licking the same juices that had caused her illness, but I know of no evidence that this had even occurred to the author. The poem, like so many poems, must be described as an open-ended allegory, 'teasing us out of thought', obviously meaning more than it says, but obviously not meaning any of the specific readings that get imposed on it.

Goblin Market is intolerant of fixed interpretation; it is also Christina Rossetti's finest and most celebrated poem: who can (as a reader) resist those goblins?

> Laughed every goblin
> When they spied her peeping:
> Came towards her hobbling,
> Flying, running, leaping,
> Puffing and blowing,
> Chuckling, clapping, crowing,
> Clucking and gobbling,
> Mopping and mowing,
> Full of airs and graces,

Pulling wry faces,
Demure grimaces,
Cat–like and rat–like,
Snail–paced in a hurry . . .

Is this Laura or Lizzie they are mobbing? We cannot tell, since temptation is temptation, energy is energy, regardless of whether the temptation is going to succeed. (It is actually Lizzie, and the temptation will fail, but we don't yet know.) Descriptions like this, one feels, could go on for ever: the energy of the little men seems to generate a corresponding energy in the language (though in truth it is, of course, the other way round).

Rossetti wrote nothing else like *Goblin Market*, and nothing which quite so teasingly resists interpretation, but she wrote several poems in which sexual betrayal and religion encounter each other – indeed, it can perhaps be described as her main theme. One of the strangest is *The Convent Threshold,* one of the strangest poems by a 19th century woman: religious and sexual, powerful and confusing, frank and evasive. The speaker is a fallen woman about to enter a convent, who addresses her now rejected lover:

There's blood between us, love, my love,
There's father's blood, there's brother's blood;
And blood's a bar I cannot pass:
I choose the stairs that mount above,
Stair after golden skyward stair.

The melodramatic references to 'father's blood, brother's blood' are never explained: they seem to hint at a story like that of Tennyson's *Maud*, in which the heroine's brother is actually killed by her lover, but the narrative of this poem is never coherent enough for us to construct the story. Dodging in and out of narrative coherence is one of the most prominent characteristics of modernism, yet this poem does not feel modernist at all: its incoherence is bewildering and moving, yet never seems to offer a subversive attitude towards narrative itself.

The references to blood recur later, and remain puzzling. She recalls her last night's dream, in which he stood by her bed and asked 'Do you dream of me?' She answered 'half asleep':

My pillow is damp, my sheets are red,
There's a leaden tester to my bed:
Find you a warmer playfellow,
A warmer pillow for your head,
A kinder love to love than mine.'
You wrung your hands; while I like lead
Crushed downwards thro' the sodden earth:
You smote your hands but not in mirth,
And reeled but were not drunk with wine.

Strange and moving dream, despite the cliché of the last line. A dream of renunciation more intensely passionate than consummation, containing another strange image of blood: were her sheets red with menstrual blood, had she wounded herself in her grief, or is it imagined blood – and if so, are the associations sexual or wounding, or both?

Like so many fallen women in Victorian literature, the speaker repents, intensely, even luridly – but repentance is not often so deeply blended with continued desire as here. The intensity of her renunciation leaves her like an old woman ('My face was pinched, my hair was grey'); if he could see her he would ask 'Where is the face I used to love?', which leads into her upbeat answer, that they will meet in heaven, thus ending the poem on a positive, hopeful note:

There we shall meet as once we met
And love with old familiar love.

Positive, upbeat? But has this ending not given away the truth that the rest of the poem denies? If they meet in heaven it has to be because they have both repented, that their love is now sanctified, that it is anything but the 'old familiar love' of their sinful days: but the conclusion appears to claim that it still is. Seldom does a poem of repentance give itself away so disastrously as this.

Did Christina Rossetti know what she was doing? Did she notice that instead of writing 'with sanctified and purer love' – the wish of the repentant sinner who longs for her lover to share her repentance – she has ended by revealing that the repentance is a mere shell and the love endures as it was. The poem has betrayed the poet.

Rossetti's most personal narrative poem is probably *Twice*, which fits the facts of her life better than any other. The first three of its six stanzas tell how she 'took her heart in her hand', and offered it to a man, who took it with 'a friendly smile', scanned it 'with a critical eye', and 'set it down'; it broke, she managed to smile in return,

> But I have not often smiled
>   Since then, nor questioned since,
> Nor cared for cornflowers wild
>   Nor sung with the singing bird.

The other three stanzas now turn to the present tense, and describe offering the heart that was 'contemned of a man' once again, this time to God:

> I take my heart in my hand –
>   I shall not die but live –
> Before Thy face I stand;
>   I, for Thou callest such:
> All that I have I bring,
>   All that I am I give,
> Smile Thou and I shall sing,
>   But shall not question much.

It is a cry of pain, followed by a cry of faith, and faith is perhaps most believable when it emerges from pain. We need not worry unduly whether the reader shares the faith: to be moved by the poem is not to be convinced that God has accepted the gift, but to be convinced that she believes He has.

'This contemned of a man': the question that we have learnt to put aside when reading older texts – the question whether *man* means 'human being' or 'male human being' – is for once important for this poem. The word depends for its power on precisely that verbal element which feminism has taught us to be uneasy with. Of course 'man' is here contrasted with God, but the gender is certainly not irrelevant.

Twice is a poem about transference. That of course is a technical term from psycho-analysis, and we can here use the word in something very close to its technical meaning: the emotion that was thwarted in the human relationship is transferred to God the analyst, who now turns out to be reliable as the human lover wasn't. Both God and the analyst are authority figures: the transference succeeds because it invests such a figure with love. To love and submit – to transfer affection to a figure who retains our respect and whose power over us we recognise – produces the formula that both psycho-analysis and Christianity demand. (In psycho-analysis one more stage is needed, detaching the transference, so that the patient is no longer reliant on the analyst, but this of course does not occur in the case of God.) There is no doubt that *Twice* is based on a recognition of this: the repetition of *judge* in stanza 4, and the joyous acceptance of the last line of the poem, are clear evidence of submission to authority. The poem could be called 'How she fell in love with God'.

One further question can occur to the modern reader: does a poem like this have to be spoken by a woman about a man, or can the authority figure be seen as female? Perhaps the answer, in our society, has to be No – or at any rate, not yet. I say 'our society', assuming that on this point there has not been all that much change since 1864. Or has there? In a world of women judges, women soldiers and women prime ministers (including, in the case of Britain, a strikingly authoritarian one) it is at least worth asking whether the assumption that authority figures are male has begun to weaken. I can think of no better way to test this than to try reading this poem (making the necessary changes of pronoun) on the assumption that it is spoken by a man. Of course such an exercise would have astonished and perhaps horrified its author.

Rossetti's best known poems are of course the short ones: in an age of anthologies, this is inevitable; and the crystalline purity of some of her short lyrics means that they clearly deserve their fame. Here are two of the most famous: first, her most famous sonnet:

> Remember me when I am gone away,
>   Gone far away into the silent land;
>   When you can no more hold me by the hand,
> Nor I half turn to go, yet turning stay.
> Remember me when no more day by day
>   You tell me of our future that you planned;
>   Only remember me: you understand
> It will be late to counsel then or pray.
> Yet if you should forget me for a while
>   And afterwards remember, do not grieve:
>   For if the darkness and corruption leave
> A vestige of the thoughts that once I had,
> Better by far you should forget and smile
>   Than that you should remember and be sad.

The poem is clear and direct and needs no interpretation; but there are two ways of discussing it, depending on what context we put it in. There is, first, the biographical context: who is she writing to? In one sense, there is no need to answer this: the reader can substitute her own 'you', and regard the poem as written to the man of her own choice. But there is no end to biographical curiosity, and there will always be readers who want to know whether it is addressed to James Collinson, to whom she was engaged in 1848 (her brother dates the poem to 1849). Her engagement to Collinson was an on-off affair, because of his religious vacillation (she felt she could not marry a Roman Catholic), and it is difficult to fit the feeling of the poem onto her life, since it seems to be about her literally dying, not about belief interfering with love. Indeed, the poem could be an illustration of how biographical readings can do more harm than good to our response, pointing us in quite a different direction from the poem.

But if we relate it not to her life but to the poem from which it seems to derive, we find a much more helpful context. That poem is Shakespeare's Sonnet no. 71:

> No longer mourn for me when I am dead
> Than you shall hear the surly sullen bell
> Give warning to the world that I am fled
> From this vile world with vilest worms to dwell . . .

The parallel here is so close that it is difficult not to believe that she had Shakespeare's poem in mind. In both of them the speaker thinks about his/her own death, and urges the friend/lover not to grieve. There are differences, but the very closeness of the two situations throws the differences into relief. Rossetti begins by saying the opposite to Shakespeare ('remember me'/ 'remember not'), but when she turns to 'Yet' in the sestet she leaves the impression that from the beginning she had felt unselfish enough to want him to forget her if remembering would cause him to 'be sad'. And this very shift determines what is really the central difference between the two poems, the fact that hers is much less religious than Shakespeare's. Her poem is really concerned only with the survivor's feelings, and her wish that he should 'forget and smile' is entirely what she wishes now, with no suggestion that her surviving soul will be thinking of him then. The Shakespeare sonnet of course also has no reference to immortality, but its world is 'this vile world', its death-bell is 'surly', and it seems imbued with some of the contempt for the world that at least ultimately derives from Christianity.

We know that Rossetti was deeply and conventionally religious, and no one knows, or ever will know, what Shakespeare's deep personal beliefs were like. If it then surprises us to find something like Christian melancholy in his poem and no touch of it in hers, that simply tells us how little the crudeness of biography can tell us about the depths of the creative self. As we could also discover by thinking about *Uphill*.

This poem looks forward to the fact that death will bring rest:

> Shall I find comfort, travel sore and weak?
>   Of labour you shall find the sum.
> Will there be beds for me and all who seek?
>   Yea, beds for all who come.

I used to show this poem to students and ask them about the beliefs it assumed: without fail, they told me that it is a Christian poem, that looks forward to life after death. They said this whether or not they knew who the author was, or what her beliefs were, and so when I told them that its author was deeply religious they naturally felt they were right. But the life after death it looks forward to is not of reward or punishment, not of union with God, but simply of rest – and rest available to everyone. Does this make it an atheistic poem?

Perhaps the most scholarly of Rossetti's modern critics, Jerome McGann, has advanced a fascinating way to resolve this. Rossetti, he claims, believed in the doctrine of 'Soul Sleep', that between individual death and the final day of Judgement, the soul continues in a state of sleep or suspension. She may well have held this belief, and it does fit some of her poems (though by no means all of those cited by McGann). And it does fit *Uphill*, in the sense that the bed at the end of the poem could be the soul sleep from which the Christian awakes to the Day of Judgement. Could be.

> Where shall I halt to deliver
>   This luggage I'd life set down?
> Not Thames, not Teme is the river,
>   Nor London nor Knighton the town:
>
> 'Tis a long way further than Knighton,
>   A quieter place than Clun,
> Where doomsday may thunder and lighten
>   And little 'twill matter to one.

A. E. Housman was about as atheistic as one can be, and his beliefs – or his lack of belief – would have horrified Christina Rossetti: but her poem is startlingly like his: both offer sleep after toil, with no mention of subsequent awakening. This is not, of course, to say that her Christianity was not genuine, perhaps not even that it was not deep; but it says that poems may not conform to what we know the poet believed, for we can never be sure where poems come from.

Note   The most convenient edition of Rossetti's poems is probably the Everyman *Poems and Prose,* edited by Jan March, 1994. Jerome McGann's article on 'The Religious Poetry of Christina Rossetti' appeared in *Critical Inquiry* no. 10 (September 1983).

Three Radicals

This section deals with three female poets of the later 19th century whose ideas I find sympathetic, and anyone should find interesting. The first, Augusta Webster, has already appeared in the discussion of fallen women.

Augusta Webster

A Castaway may be her finest poem, but there are other fine ones. The best of them are dramatic monologues in blank verse, the speakers being usually women, sometimes mythical or fictitious figures from the past, rather more often contemporaries. I will begin with what may be the best of the myths, the poem on *Circe*. In Homer, Circe is an enchantress who turns Odysseus' men into swine by offering them her magic cup to drink, and like so many enchantresses in Greek mythology she is both goddess and woman: when Odysseus outwits her she becomes his mistress and bears him a son. Webster was not very interested in goddesses, and her Circe is very human, longing for a lover:

> Oh love, oh love, oh love, art not yet come
> Out of the waiting shadows into life?
> Art not yet come out of so many years
> That I have longed for thee? Come, I am here.

But she has only the company of those she has turned into beasts, 'these bestial things / Who wallow in their styes / . . . These things who had believed that they were men.' The Homeric tale of magic here becomes a moral fable: Circe's victims are turned into beasts because their natures were bestial. She takes no pleasure in her powers, but will 'sickly look and loathe them all'.

Webster's Circe is steeped in Tennyson: the approaching storm will toss down

> My riotous vines with their young half-tinged grapes
> like small round amethysts or beryls strung
> tumultuously in clusters,

and will make

> . . . my pleached and mossy labyrinths,
> where the small odorous blossoms grow like stars
> strewn in the milky way, a briny marsh.

The verbal skin is magnificent, though it has not (so far) kept Webster's poems afloat in the sea of time: I hope that by quoting enough I can help to remedy this.

The poem ends with a storm approaching, and the reader who knows the story realises (though of course Circe doesn't) that it is about to wreck Odysseus on her island. She concludes: 'It were well / I bade make ready for our guests tonight.' On one level, this is a simple irony: the 'guest' will be Odysseus, who will resist her magic, and become her lover. But to read this as irony at Circe's expense would be too simple: she has been sympathetically presented as an angry woman, and her adventure with Odysseus will, in the end, do nothing to cure her anger.

This Circe sounds very like a modern woman; and Webster's best monologues are put in the mouth of contemporaries: perhaps her most fascinating poem of contemporary life, after *A Castaway,* is *Tired.* Here the speaker is a man who has married an unsophisticated country girl because he

> mistook the freedom of blunt ignorance
> for one with freedom of the instructed will.

Madge, the wife, was not naïve of deliberate purpose, and so when she married into society she set out to shed her country ways and become sophisticated. How can he tell her this was not what he had in mind? Out of kindness he is careful not to let his wife know that he made a mistake:

> mistake − 'tis a hard word. Well let it pass:

it shall not wrong her: for was it in her
or in myself I was mistaken most?

So he sends her out for the social evening she is eager for, knowing she will soon get over her disappointment that he is not coming, congratulating her on the sophisticated costume he would prefer her not to wear, and telling himself – and her – that he is too tired to come. While she is dressing he reflects not only on the marriage, but on what he has done with his life: he has been a well meaning reformer who cannot escape from the realisation that society has not really got any better:

> Most horrible days; and we who know the worst,
> (or dream it, sitting in our easy chairs,
> sorry that all men have not easy chairs,)
> and would do somewhat, do it all amiss.

The vagueness with which the ills of society are probed ('the cavernous cry / Of shame and ignorance, hunger and greed') contrasts strongly with the shrewd probing of his own ineffectiveness: the poem is about him, not about the problems of Victorian England. His reverie is interrupted by Madge's return, dressed for the party, and concludes with his sad kindly affection.

Angela Leighton has done more for Victorian women poets than anyone, so if I now enter a disagreement with her reading of this poem it is not to cavil, but to explore the nature of the dramatic monologue. When the speaker is clearly not the poet herself, we are inevitably offered a blend of identification and irony, and there is always the possibility that different readers will see the blending differently: is Browning's *Andrea del Sarto,* for instance, a picture of sad, clear-sighted self-knowledge, or an ironic picture of self-deception? The speaker of *Tired* has much in common with Browning's Andrea, and Leighton's reading of the poem sees him as self-deceiving: 'his eloquent anger about women's roles seems designed to comfort his solitude and confirm his liberalism rather than to address the specific situation of Madge.'

Readers will obviously decide for themselves how to interpret *Tired*: as a portrait of a self-deceiving liberal, or (as I believe) of sad self-knowledge; but I believe it important to maintain that either extreme is possible in a poem, and neither is necessarily preferable to the other: the dramatic monologue can stretch from the almost pure irony of (say) Browning's *Soliloquy of the Spanish Cloister* to the almost pure identification of Tennyson's *Ulysses*. The temperament and opinions of a reader will no doubt influence where she places a particular monologue on this scale; but I think it important to say that it is not compulsory for the poem to be ironic at the speaker's expense. The monologue of sad self-knowledge is a possibility, and is one that Webster was often drawn to.

As, for instance, in *A Soul in Prison*: not one of her most powerful monologues, but one with which the agnostic reader cannot but sympathise. The speaker is a 'doubter' who has just read, and been disappointed by, a book of Christian apologetics, which has told him 'There are ledges somewhere by which strong feet / Might scale to daylight' but when he responds 'I find no ledges' it proposes wilfulness as the explanation. This poem makes one point only: that the orthodox treat honest doubt with less understanding than they treat sinners – and makes it shrewdly. Since the book he has read set out to cure him of unbelief he offers a parallel with a doctor who 'cured' in the same way:

> My doctor tells me 'Why, quite long ago
> They knew your fever (or one very like);
> And they knew remedies, you'll find them named
> In many ancient writers, let those serve';
> And 'Thick on the commons, by the daily roads,
> The herbs are growing that give instant strength
> To palsied limbs like yours, clear such filmed sight:
> You need but eyes to spy them, hands to uproot,
> That's all.'

To which the speaker replies '*All*, truly.' We know little about Augusta Webster's life, rather more about her opinions, because of her modestly titled book *A Housewife's Opinions*, and there seems little doubt that she felt very close to this 'doubter'.

As she seems to me very close to the speaker of *Tired*, who is conducting a dialogue not with the imagined author of the book he is reading, but with himself: a self who began by answering 'the clamorous call of new crusades' and now sits

> A weary man growing old
> among the ruin of his purposes
> hopeless of any good to be by him.

The two themes, that of the disillusioned idealist and the husband who made a 'mistake', but loving his wife manages to conceal it from her, join to make a sad, unironic, moving poem.

Webster had one child, Margaret, who became an actress, and took part in the one of her mother's plays which is known to have reached the stage; and her last book of poems, published posthumously, was an unfinished sonnet-sequence, *Mother & Daughter*. It makes a natural comparison with George Eliot's sonnet sequence *Brother & Sister*: both were written much later than the events they describe, both are filled with happy domestic affection, and neither could be claimed as among the author's best work. But at least they illustrate the Proustian truth, that the most moving literature tends to be about loss: in George Eliot's case, she wrote the sonnets after her brother had disowned her, and in Webster's case, though she remained close to her daughter, she had lost, as all mothers do, the dependence of the infant:

> I miss the approaching sound of pit-pat feet,
> The eager baby voice outside my door.

Mathilde Blind

If we yield to the temptation to judge those who lived in the past by the criteria of the present, then there is surely no Victorian woman more interesting and more attractive than Mathilde Blind, who was neither prudish, provincial, monoglot, timid, conventional or ignorant. Her parents were German political refugees, her life was adventurous (her solitary walking tour in Switzerland was undertaken with no resources, and she had to be persuaded out of extending it to the Caucasus), and she mixed with radicals and sceptics: she was a lifelong admirer of Mazzini and George Eliot, a friend of Ford Madox Brown, and a keen supporter of women's education, leaving most of her estate to Newnham College. And she wrote poetry: several volumes of very competent lyrics, and three long poems.

The lyrics do not differ greatly from plenty of other competent 19th century poems, but the long poems are striking for their choice of subjects. *The Prophecy of St Oran* retells a medieval Scottish legend in which a young and saintly monk sins with a young woman, eventually confesses, and is killed by order of St Columba: a conventional enough Christian legend, except that the young monk stands up in his grave to tell his brothers that there is no God, that they should 'Cast down the crucifix, take up the plough / Nor waste your breath which is the life in prayer'; but St Columba, 'white with Christian ire', orders him to be reburied, 'That his blaspheming tongue may blab no more.' That is the last line of the poem, which ends not with a conventionally Christian resolution, nor with the triumph of Oran's defiance, but with the monks reasserting their curse: presumably to remind us that conventional Christianity continued to hold power for a long time.

The Heather on Fire tells the story of the Highland clearances with fierce radical indignation, in which virtuous peasants are expelled by ruthless landlords; and the third and most ambitious of her long poems, *The Ascent of Man* tells the story of humanity, and was reissued after her death with a preface by Alfred Russell Wallace. It is a blend of Shelleyan visions and scientific realism, though the science, inevitably, now seems rather outdated to us.

> War rages on the teeming earth;
>   The hot and sanguinary fight
> Begins with each new creature's birth:
>   A dreadful war where might is right:
> Where still the strongest slay and win,
> Where weakness is the only sin.

That is a not untypical stanza. A scientific account of the ascent of man will obviously not be in moral terms, and in the struggle for existence might obviously is right: but what makes such an account scientific is ignoring moral issues as irrelevant to its mode of study, not constant reminders of how wicked the whole process is if we apply moral criteria. It is not easy to know how far Blind's vision is horrified by or is taking a grim satisfaction in the absence of morality as humanity struggles upwards. Indeed, despite the poem's title, it is not at all clear that the struggle is upward. Part III of the poem is actually called 'The Leading of Sorrow', and promises sight of 'the awful reaper / Evil, reaping all beneath the sun.' Although it ends with an assertion about 'Love re-arisen / With the Eternal shining through his eyes', that uplifting conclusion is tacked on to some very gloomy writing, including assertions like

> Life is but a momentary blunder
>   In the eyes of all the Universe

If we were to change *blunder* to, say, 'accident', this might well be the opinion of a modern cosmologist: we'd lose the rhyme with 'asunder', but to the modern reader this might count as a gain. Indeed, what might strike a modern reader most in this poem is the constant and varied competence of its versifying. Blind's mastery of rhyme and metre is very accomplished, and she does what authors of long poems seldom do, which is to switch, as section follows section, from one rhyme scheme and metrical pattern to another, deploying some often complicated stanza patterns with great competence. Is this an advantage in a long poem? It might lead us, on the contrary, to sympathise with Milton's bad-tempered prefatory note to *Paradise Lost*, that rhyme 'is the invention of a barbarous age to set off wretched matter and lame metre'. There is no timeless answer to this question, since poetry readers today, though they may vary in how much they enjoy rhyme and regular metre, hardly ever expect it in the way earlier readers did. Metrical patterning is no longer considered necessary, and may even, to the modern reader, feel like unnecessary baggage that needs to be shed.

Since Blind is little read today, and not easily obtainable, we ought to look at a complete poem: so here is a sonnet, called *The Red Sunsets*.

The twilight heavens are flushed with gathering light,
    And o'er wet roofs and huddling streets below
    Hang with a strange Apocalyptic glow
On the black fringes of the wintry night.
Such bursts of glory may have rapt the sight
    Of him to whom on Patmos long ago
    The visionary angel came to show
That heavenly city built of chrysolite;
And lo, three factory hands begrimed with soot,
    Aflame with the red splendour, marvelling stand,
And gaze with lifted faces awed and mute,
  Starved of earth's beauty by man's grudging hand,
O toilers, robbed of labour's golden fruit,
    Ye too may feast in Nature's fairyland.

This is certainly a poem with a message: the beauty of the sunset may once have charmed John on Patmos, now it charms three deprived factory hands. What then is the relation between its opening description and its political conclusion? Is it a Christian socialist poem: the vision of John provides a template for the joy of those whom society deprives? Or is it an anti-Christian poem: sunsets used to be seen as heavenly visions, now we see them as the one form of beauty available to the poor? We know enough about Blind to say with confidence that the latter is a more likely reading (though she did have an intensely religious phase, so we cannot be sure – and perhaps she couldn't either). If we cannot be sure, is that to the poem's discredit? Probably not: the contrast between the two ways of regarding the sunset could provide the power of the poem, without requiring us to choose which moral we draw. But does the poem moralise about the sunset instead of responding to it? It was written only a decade or two later than Baudelaire's *Crepuscule du Soir*, in which the evening, friend of the criminal, 'vient comme un complice, à pas de loup': the magic of this makes her description seem trite. Why? Of course such questions are not easy to answer, perhaps too subtle to answer at all. Certainly Blind's factory hands are rather predictably 'grimed with soot' just as their lifted faces are, quite as predictably, 'awed and mute'; and the rhetorical gesture of addressing the three workmen seems stiff and even theatrical. Baudelaire's opening gesture of calling the evening 'le soir charmant, ami du criminel' has an impudence that makes Blind's worthy political point seem ponderous.

But is it unfair to choose a poem with a political moral: should we not give Blind a chance simply to capture experience? Another sonnet describes sunset, this time in the Alps, and gives it a more purely personal application:

The After-Glow

It is a solemn evening, golden-clear –
  The Alpine summits flame with rose-lit snow
  And headlands purpling on wide seas below,
And clouds and woods and arid rocks appear
Dissolving in the sun's own atmosphere
  And vast circumference of light, whose slow
  Transfiguration – glow and after-glow –
Turns twilight earth to a more luminous sphere.

Oh heart, I ask, seeing that the orb of day
Has sunk below, yet left to sky and sea
  His glory's spiritual after-shine:
I ask if Love, whose sun hath set for thee,
May not touch grief with his memorial ray,
  And lend to loss itself a joy divine.

Blind was a lifelong enthusiast for Shelley, to whom the first, descriptive part of this sonnet surely owes a lot (though the first line perhaps remembers Wordsworth's famous opening, 'It is a beauteous evening, calm and free'); without the Romantic poets we would never have had the visible details 'Dissolving in the sun's own atmosphere / And vast circumference of light', surely the finest touch in the poem. The poet must have felt that the hushed awe of the octave needed a moralising conclusion, and this time, avoiding politics, she offers a dutiful parallel with love and grief. But has personal emotion served her much better than political idealism?

Amy Levy

Amy Levy grew up a Jew, wrote about Jewish themes, and was sometimes attacked in Jewish circles for her less than complimentary picture of Jewish culture – especially (but perhaps rather unjustly) after the publication of her novel of Jewish life, *Reuben Sachs*. Intensely conscious of radical opinion and of her Jewish heritage, probably lesbian and certainly feminist, she was a student at Newnham (its first Jewish student); admired and was friendly with both radicals (Eleanor Marx and Olive Schreiner) and the 'decadents' (Vernon Lee and Oscar Wilde). She had published three novels and three volumes of poetry by the time she committed suicide at the age of 28.

Like Augusta Webster (perhaps in imitation of her) she wrote a poem about Medea: the woman in Greek legend who married and was betrayed by Jason and took the terrible revenge of murdering their children seems to have haunted several late Victorian poets. Levy's Medea is less frightening than Webster's, and is rather ponderously antique in diction, with too many lines like 'I wax white and do tremble'. Much more contemporary is her poem about a suicide, *A Minor Poet*, which may have been prompted by the suicide of James Thomson, author of *The City of Dreadful Night*, the unhappiest of all late Victorian poets in both his life and his work. The poem refers to Thomson – without naming him – as 'one wild singer of today . . . Lashed into foam by pain and the world's wrong', as one more fortunate than the speaker because at least 'he has a voice to cry his pain', but this need not exclude the possibility that he was a model for the protagonist; though no doubt the other model was Levy herself. Though free of the ponderous archaising of *Medea*, it has its own rather ponderous gloom ('For all the sunset glory, Pain is king') as well as some Malthusian pessimism ('In troop the guests, each with an appetite . . . What's this? What's this? There are not seats for all!'). Both ancient and modern themes seem to hold dangers for this poet.

Her best poem seems to me to be *Xantippe*, a subject that one can see was waiting for an intelligent feminist to find it. Xantippe was the wife of Socrates, whom legend represented as a shrew. Why? Nothing is known about her, and it seems a likely guess that such a legend owes more to the assumptions of those among whom it arose than to any independent evidence: to burden this heroic philosopher with domestic trials is a way of reminding us that the wisest men are not free of burdens. But why this particular burden? If we shift our attention from Socrates himself to the wife, there is the more obvious point that ancient Athenian society excluded women. Levy's Xantippe is an idealistic young woman who had admired Socrates and was delighted to find she was to marry him (not of course making the choice herself, but still delighted) – only to find that he did not see himself as marrying a companion, but rather a servant. So she narrates a scene in which Xantippe, bringing the men a fresh wine-skin, suddenly ('lit by a fury and a thought') intervenes in their discussion with an indignant defence of women. Plato and Alcibiades are amused but her husband is scornful:

> I thank thee for the wisdom which thy lips
> Have thus let fall among us: prythee tell
> From what high source, from what philosophies
> Didst cull the sapient notion of thy words?

Socrates' method was to begin discussions from first principles rather than cite authorities. His put-down of Xantippe is that she is too ignorant to be able to cite authorities: masculine self-assurance blinding him to his inconsistency. Of course Levy invented this episode: but then who invented the legend that Xantippe was a shrew?

Magdalen, a short narrative about a woman dying, probably in the workhouse, is a typical example of Levy's realism and her gloom (and perhaps her limitations). The title does not indicate a religious theme, *Magdalen* being used simply to mean 'fallen woman'. The narrative is minimal: she remembers a love affair in which she had been happy, and declares that she would have given him up if she had been told 'A poison lurks within your kiss', but whether it did is not made clear. Was she a prostitute briefly redeemed, or an innocent woman corrupted, by the man she loved? Levy's interest is not in the details of the narrative, but in the sufferings of the woman:

> . . . in a hideous masquerade
> All things dance on, the ages through,
> And good is evil, evil good;
> Nothing is known or understood.

Such a poem perhaps illustrates Levy's depressiveness at the expense of her intelligence, so it is a relief to find her being witty about the social and intellectual change she was so involved with. *A Ballad of Religion and*

Marriage asks if the conventions of marriage depend on those of religion, and since the latter have gone, 'Shall marriage go the way of God?'

> Monogamous, still at our post,
>   Reluctantly we undergo
> Domestic round of boiled and roast,
>   Yet deem the whole proceeding slow.
> Daily the secret murmurs grow;
>   We are no more content to plod
> Along the beaten paths – and so
>   Marriage must go the way of God.

Verse, not poetry, certainly: but for verse as entertaining as this, we would forego many a conventional poem.

Two of the most famous remarks about the nature and value of poetry were made by Frenchmen: Mallarmé's observation to Degas that poetry is not made out of ideas but out of words, and Gide's observation that a masterpiece is kept afloat in the sea of time because of its skin, by which he meant much the same: that poetic value depends not on the ideas but on the words in which they are wrapped. How far ideas and the language that wraps them can be separated is a question that will continue to exercise philosophers of language, but however dubious the philosophic underpinning, the distinction is one that corresponds to something in our experience, and will continue to be made. For those interested in nineteenth century women's poetry, there is a particularly striking example:

> Give me your tired, your poor,
> Your huddled masses yearning to breathe free,
> The wretched refuse of your teeming shore.
> Send these, the homeless, tempest tossed to me,
> I lift my lamp beside the golden door!

These are probably the most widely read lines of poetry by any 19th century woman, yet their author is virtually forgotten. They are the concluding lines of the sonnet by Emma Lazarus carved on the pedestal of the Statue of Liberty. Their sentiment is generous and splendid, and embodies the open door policy of the United States till the MacLaren Act was passed and put a stop to it. Poetically, they are undistinguished, the adjectives are trite and obvious, but they have stirred the hearts of millions. To judge them as poetry is not the same as to judge them morally – or politically.

And these three women, rich in generous and forward looking ideas? They were not fortunate enough to have their poems carved on a great monument; looking back at them from a later age, in which many of their aspirations have been realised, we can place them in the development of thought by saying they were followers of Strauss and Darwin, Mill and Mazzini, rather than of Carlyle and Mr Gladstone, and that they anticipated much of our own time. But they were all poets, so what about the words? Will their works be kept afloat by their skin?

The poems of Blind and Levy will not: they seem to me significant figures in social and intellectual history, rather than in the history of poetry. Far more intelligent and interesting than Christina Rossetti, they were not capable of writing anything as moving as *Twice* or as magical as *Goblin Market*. That does not mean they are not worth reading, simply that we read them for different reasons. Augusta Webster, the least flamboyant of the three, was easily the finest poet. In her case, the neglect she has fallen into is disgraceful and should be remedied. She is a clear case (to revert to the categories proposed in my Introduction) for individual recuperation: the best of her dramatic monologues can stand beside Browning's, and need no special pleading, no adjusting of criteria.

Note   Much the most convenient way to read these three poets is in *Out of my Borrowed Books: Poems by AW, MB and AL*, edited by Judith Willson (Carcanet 2006).

Emily Dickinson

'The old words are numb,' wrote Dickinson to Samuel Bowles in 1852, 'and there a'nt any *new* ones.' To some extent, this is the problem of any poet; and the more it is felt as a problem, the more the poet will be driven to unorthodoxy and experiment. Emily Dickinson, the timid, solitary New England spinster, is probably the greatest, and certainly the most experimental, of all the women poets in the language, and her poems struggle to use the old words as if they really were new ones.

Her story is almost as strange as one of her poems. When Mabel Loomis Todd came to live in Amherst, she wrote a description of her which has become famous, and which no retelling can improve on:

I must tell you about the character of Amherst. It is a lady whom the people call the Myth. She is the sister of Mr Dickinson, and seems to be the climax of all the family oddity. She has not been outside of her own house in fifteen years, except once to see a new church, when she crept out at night, and viewed it by moonlight. No-one who calls upon her mother and sister ever see her, but she allows little children once in a great while, and one at a time, to come in, when she gives them cake or candy, or some nicety, for she is very fond of little ones. But more often she lets down the sweetmeat by a string, out of a window, to them. She dresses wholly in white, and her mind is said to be perfectly wonderful. She writes finely, but no-one ever sees her . . . Isn't that like a book? So interesting

Todd was probably referring to her letters when she remarked 'she writes finely', for Dickinson was a passionate correspondent; but it was not altogether a secret that she wrote poetry, and she often included a poem in a letter to a friend.

Her one approach to the public literary world came in 1862, when she was 31: she wrote to Colonel Thomas William Higginson, a well-known freelance writer, enclosing four of her poems, and asking 'Are you too deeply occupied to say if my verse is alive?' She was sufficiently encouraged by his reply to send three more in a second letter, and the ensuing correspondence continued intermittently until her death. She always refused to come to Worcester to see him ('I do not cross my father's ground to any house or town'), and eventually he called on her at Amherst: the account of her which he sent his wife makes a good parallel to Todd's:

A step like a pattering child's in the entry, and in glided a little plain woman with two smooth bands of reddish hair . . . in a very plain exquisitely clean white pique and a blue net worsted shawl. She came to me with two day lilies which she put in a sort of childlike way into my hand and said 'These are my introduction' in a soft frightened breathless childlike voice . . . '

He then added a few of her remarks, including 'My father only reads on Sunday – he reads *lonely and rigorous* books' and 'I find ecstasy in living – the mere sense of living is joy enough'. Nervous as she was, she managed to say 'many thing which you would have thought foolish and I wise'. Higginson's conventional literary taste was, not surprisingly, uneasy with the radical experimentalism of her poems, but he clearly

responded both to her charm and their power. After her death, he and
Mabel Loomis Todd published a selection of the poems, and his preface
indicates his mixed but appreciative response:

> In many cases these verses will seem to the reader like poetry torn up by
> the roots, with rain and dew and earth still clinging to them, giving a
> freshness and a fragrance not otherwise to be conveyed. In other cases,
> as in a few poems of shipwreck or of mental conflict, we can only wonder
> at the gift of vivid imagination by which this recluse woman can delin-
> eate, by a few touches, the very crises of physical and mental struggle.

Discussion of her poems can begin almost anywhere. Most poets
write poems of varying length, on a range of subjects, and publish them
from time to time in volumes. Dickinson wrote 1775 short poems,
without titles, and published virtually none of them. There is little or
no change of style or subject over the years, and attempts to classify her
poems by subject – love, religion, nature, introspection – soon run into
confusion because of the way one subject fuses into another. Let us
begin with a poem which clearly tries to treat the old words as if they
were new:

> If you were coming in the Fall,
> I'd brush the summer by
> With half a smile, and half a spurn,
> As Housewives do, a Fly.
>
> If I could see you in a year,
> I'd wind the months in balls –
> And put them each in separate Drawers,
> For fear the numbers fuse –
>
> If only Centuries, delayed,
> I'd count them on my Hand.
> Subtracting, till my fingers dropped
> Into Van Diemens land.
>
> If certain, when this life was out –
> That yours and mine, should be
> I'd toss it yonder, like a Rind,
> And take Eternity –

> But now, uncertain of the length
> Of this, that is between,
> It goads me, like the Goblin Bee –
> That will not state – its sting.   (511)

Both style and subject are striking. The subject is huge, and is expressed sometimes through quaintly far-fetched images, and sometimes through homely domestic detail, in a manner reminiscent of the religious poems of George Herbert ('who sweeps a room as for thy laws Makes that and th'action fine'). The homely details are never straightforward: the months are put away in drawers with mothballs 'for fear the numbers fuse': both of the last two words, in different ways, attack the numbness of ordinary language, thrusting in a touch of abstraction or a different metaphor. This thrusting in of the unexpected begins in the very first stanza: 'With half a smile and half a frown' is what we would expect, and instead we get not only a different contrast to 'smile', but a grammatical shock too, since 'spurn' is normally a verb, though it sounds English enough to use it here as a substantive. Similarly with the bee in the last stanza: are bees compared to goblins because of their unpredictability, or is this a *goblin* bee as contrasted with an ordinary bee? If it will not 'state its sting', does that mean it does not actually sting, or that it does not tell us when or how severely (or even whether) it is going to sting? The answer to these questions is that it could be either: the language is as elusive as the situation.

This elusiveness in the writing is matched by a central ambiguity in the subject: who is being addressed – God, or a lover? This is not an unusual situation in Dickinson's poems, which tell frequently of a relationship with a 'he' who seems sometimes divine, sometimes human:

> My worthiness is all my Doubt –
> His Merit – all my fear –
> Contrasting which, my quality
> Do lowlier – appear –
>
> Lest I should insufficient prove
> For His beloved Need –
> The Chiefest Apprehension
> Upon my thronging Mind –
>
> 'Tis true – that Deity to stoop
> Inherently incline –

For nothing higher than Itself
Itself can rest upon –

So I – the undivine abode
Of his Elect content –
Conform my Soul – as 'twere a Church,
Unto Her Sacrament.   (751)

The first two stanzas could be about a woman fearing that she cannot live up to the high standards of the man she loves, or a Christian worrying about being a sinner unworthy of God's love; the other two stanzas are very explicitly Christian, but this does not remove the ambiguity, since they can be read as analogy: just as the Christian's devotion is acceptable to God because He inevitably elects those who are far beneath him, so I need not worry about my insufficiency to love any man as I wish to, since all love (we have seen this topos in the Brownings already) is *from beneath*.

If we treat this ambiguity as peculiar to Dickinson, we could be tempted to look for an explanation in her life, and there has been no lack of biographers searching for a man for whom she felt unrequited love. The search takes us to, but is arrested by, three fascinating letters addressed to 'Master' which were found among her papers. We do not know if these are drafts of letters sent to a man, or sketches of possible letters never sent, or something more like diary entries. We do not know if the Master is a particular man, or someone imagined, or God – or a version of God.

Have you the Heart in your breast – sir – is it set like mine – a little to
the left – has it the misgiving –if it wake in the night – perchance – itself
to it – a timbrel is it – itself to it a tune?

The letters in fact have the same ambiguity as the poems. Indeed, they are like poems, often with the same haunting imagery: 'You send the water over the Dam in my brown eyes.'

The reason we cannot 'explain' the poems by referring to the life is of course that the life is not something directly accessible to us. We have biographical documents that on matters of fact can yield certainty enough (we know that she was born in Amherst in 1830, that her father and brother were both leading citizens of the town, that she never married, and so on), but once we turn to the really interesting and awkward questions, the documents can turn out to be as difficult to interpret as the poems.

And if some of Dickinson's finest poems read as if they could be addressed to either God or a man, we should not be surprised: for the analogy between human and divine love is central to all writing about either. Sexual love has long been considered a transfiguring of experience, different from (and superior to) all other earthly experiences, so it must inevitably be compared to the supreme example of rejecting the world for something higher. And contrariwise, if the love of God lifts us onto a higher plane than any secular experience, how better can it be described than in terms of the one secular experience that also seems to lift us onto a higher plane. The love poems of John Donne are full of religious images, and his Holy Sonnets are full of sexual analogies. This traffic between the language of the human and that of divine love goes back at least to the Middle Ages, and one of its classic expressions is Dante's *Vita Nuova*, in which the poet's love for Beatrice and his adoration of the Queen of Heaven become almost indistinguishable.

In principle, then, this mystery in Dickinson's poems (God or man?) is not unprecedented; but there are still ways in which they distinguish themselves from the tradition. First, the uncertainty is more central: we quite literally do not know, very often, whether human is being compared to divine love, or the opposite. Second, most such love/religion poems are addressed to a woman, since most love poems have been written by men; here the 'Master' is quite obviously male, and this means that these poems go even closer to the heart of the ambiguity: it is God himself, not an angel or the Virgin Mary, who forms one half of the possible meaning. And finally, there is the occasional suggestion that the Master has in some way let her down, that the love is unrequited, the faith unanswered: she 'knows that He exists' but

> Should the glee – glaze –
> In Death's – stiff – stare –
>
> Would not the fun
> Look too expensive!
> Would not the jest –
> Have crawled too far!   (338)

How powerful the emotion that can be implied by the choice of a single word, such as the – surely – resentful use of 'crawled' in the last line! As we shall shortly see, Dickinson's exploration of unrequited love and unrequited faith suggests a significant contemporary parallel.

To say one thing requires the exclusion of other meanings: that is the obvious basis of unambiguous language, such as is required in legal documents, practical life, scientific papers. Poetry in contrast makes frequent and rich use of ambiguity, but this too requires exclusion. To say two things and leave us uncertain which is intended requires the exclusion of a third or fourth possible meaning. One could even claim that to leave us hesitating between three meanings requires the exclusion of a fourth or fifth, and so on. At some point, if too many possibilities are opened up, suggestive hesitation between alternatives will turn into bewilderment, ambivalence into incomprehension, poetic richness into nonsense. To say this is not to require that poetry display the clarity of legal documents, but to perceive that poetic ambiguity is structured. Take, for example, this poem about dreaming:

> Dreams – are well – but Waking's better,
> If One wake at Morn –
> If One wake at Midnight – better –
> Dreaming – of the Dawn –
>
> Sweeter – the Surmising Robins –
> Never gladdened Tree –
> Than a Solid Dawn – confronting –
> Leading to no Day –   (450)

Poems that contrast dreams and waking could in the first, crude place be divided into those that prefer dreams (*Ode to a Nightingale, Kubla Khan*) and those that prefer waking (*Comus, Elegiac Stanzas upon Peele Castle in a Storm*). They could also be divided into those which are quite sure of their preference, and those which also imply the opposite possibility (this might include all those just mentioned). A wholly rational aesthetic – that of many 18th century critics, or of Yvor Winters – will prefer the former; most critical positions nowadays will prefer the latter.

This poem is full of uncertainties: not merely the general uncertainty about which it is preferring (is the bold assertion of the first line later undermined?) but a large number of local uncertainties. For instance, does the third line say that waking at midnight is better than waking at morn, or that waking at morn or at midnight are both better than dreams? Or that waking is better than dreaming if one wakes at morn, but if one wakes at midnight than it is better to dream of the dawn? Or even – in simple contradiction to the first line – that if one wakes at morn *or* at midnight it is better to dream of the dawn. All these readings are perfectly plausible, but can we have them all?

The second stanza, too, has ambiguities, if less radical ones than the first. In particular, whether the solid dawn confronts (and so leads to) no day, or whether 'confronting' is a verbal noun governing 'solid dawn (the robins are not sweeter than a (wakeful) confronting of solid dawn). Along with the uncertainty of 'leading to' – does it qualify 'dawn' (confronting a solid dawn which leads to no day), or is it parallel to 'confronting' (never sweeter than confronting a solid dawn or leading to no day – semantically odd but syntactically plausible), or does it qualify 'robins': the *surmising* robins belong to dream and so lead to no day – syntactically strained (though possible) but semantically plausible. And this does not exhaust the possibilities.

Dickinson's poems make wonderful use of ambiguities, but they do threaten at times to drop into bewilderment. If we ask what is the reason for this, the answer, at least in part, is the punctuation. She used hardly any punctuation except dashes. In this poem, there is one comma and thirteen dashes. In the next poem (no. 451) there are 20 dashes, 2 commas, and 2 full stops, in no. 452 there are 26 dashes, one comma and one exclamation mark. These are representative counts. The fact that she published virtually none of her poems when alive is clearly relevant here. Some regularising of punctuation was done by Higginson and Todd when they published their selection in 1890; and if a publisher had seen the poems through the press, he would certainly have required her to punctuate more conventionally. We do not of course know how she would have responded to such a requirement, just as we do not know why she only used dashes: did she despise conventional punctuation, or feel that she didn't understand it sufficiently, or consider it unnecessary in manuscripts though necessary in print? We do not know either whether the fact that her dashes are of varying length is significant or not. R. W. Franklin, who has made a thorough study of the editing of Dickinson, concludes that the use of dashes is 'a habit of her handwriting' and should not necessarily by preserved in print, especially in a 'reading edition'.

It is understandable, in these circumstances, that some should feel that Dickinson's poems need proper punctuation. John Crowe Ransom, for instance, claimed that 'she was not one of those poets who had advanced to that later stage of operations where manuscripts are prepared for the printer, and the poet's diction has to make concessions to the publisher's stylebook.' This was not the policy adopted by Thomas H Johnson in what is now the standard edition of her poems; and it is doubtful if any responsible editor would feel happy at tampering with her texts. But it is not only scholarly caution that argues against Ransom's view: there is also feminist indignation – from, for instance, Adrienne Rich:

> In short, Emily Dickinson did not wholly know her trade, and Ransom believes a 'publisher's stylebook' to have the last word on poetic diction. He goes on to print several of her poems, altered by him 'with all possible forbearance'. What might in a male writer – a Thoreau, let us say, or a Christopher Smart, or William Blake – seem a legitimate strangeness, a unique intention, has been, in one of our two major poets, devalued into a kind of naiveté, girlish ignorance, feminine lack of professionalism, just as the poet herself has been made into a sentimental object.

The controversy over Dickinson's punctuation is worth dwelling on: like so many controversies about what seems at first trivial, it can throw up genuine issues. The defenders of her dashes tend to be enthusiastic and (often) perceptive readers of her poetry, and they tend, being enthusiasts, to be unfair to their opponents. Thus Kamilla Denman, attacking Franklin's case for a 'reader's text', suggests that the editor he requires will be a 'godlike editor, critic and philosopher in one': the three nouns come from Franklin, but the adjective 'godlike' was tossed in by Denman. And Rich, too, in her otherwise splendid essay, misrepresents Ransom: to suggest changes in punctuation when manuscript turns into print is not to accuse a poet of not knowing her trade, and to feel that a publisher's stylebook has its uses is not to rate it 'the last word on poetic diction'. Published poems need to regard conventional punctuation as a norm, so that each departure from it requires a reason. Dickinson's punctuation merely flouts it.

Suppose we try, 'with all possible forbearance', to tamper with the punctuation of poem 450 ('Dreams are well but Waking's better'). We will need, first of all, to decide whether the first line should really end with a comma, or with a full stop: a full stop would make it clear that the 'if' clauses are directed forward and not backward. Deciding whether to put the third line in brackets (or the third and fourth lines), and deciding which of the dashes simply indicates a pause in the reading, and which ones mark syntactic breaks – these would not solve all our problems, and would certainly not threaten to remove the really important ambiguities: but they would help.

We do not play on Graves –
Because there isn't Room –
Besides – it isn't even – it slants
And People come –

And put a Flower on it –
And hang their faces so –
We're fearing that their Hearts will drop –
And crush our pretty play-

And so we move as far
As Enemies – away –
Just looking round to see how far
It is – Occasionally –   (467)

As far as I know there is no lengthy discussion of this poem by any of Dickinson's critics. It is not, certainly, a difficult poem, as her poems go: it has few bewildering details, but there is of course an ambiguity: is it about children playing in a churchyard, or is it about the way we avoid thinking about death? Or are these not alternatives, since the poem is an allegory?

It is often remarked that Dickinson's poems are rich in brilliant openings that are not always sustained, and the first stanza of this poem is, surely, more brilliant than anything that follows. The matter-of-fact details that describe the children playing are all deeply suggestive on the allegorical level: there 'isn't room' when the thought of death narrows and constricts our consciousness, it distorts ('slants') our thinking, it is interrupted by People (from Porlock or from our everyday life). The other two stanzas have their power too: the second contains the weirdly literal fear of the children that the mourner's 'heart will drop', and the third too has a haunting literalism as the children move as far away as they can, 'just looking round' with a child's curiosity 'to see how far it is'. All these observations about death gain their power precisely from the way we perform the mental operation of stepping into them from the poem about children playing. The poem teaches us (how often Dickinson teaches us, as we respond, how to read!) that the secret of allegory is the way it holds on to, even as it departs from, the literal event.

120

A poet who lived cut off from the world, never publishing, writing, mainly for herself alone, eccentric, unorthodox, powerful poems that look back to the past, for their wit and linguistic brilliance occasionally recall that of the metaphysical poets, and forward to the future, since once they were published posthumously they gradually made their way into prominence, and eventually became one of the central poetic forces in modernism; a poet with one literary acquaintance of comparatively conventional taste, to whom she showed her work, and who despite himself responded to and appreciated her brilliance, though he would never dream of imitating it.

Emily Dickinson? Change 'her' to 'his', and it is an account of Gerard Manley Hopkins.

The parallel between Dickinson and Hopkins can teach us a good deal about both of them, and about the nature of poetic radicalism. No-one, it is true, could ever mistake even a single line of one of them for a line by the other.

> I wake and feel the fell of dark, not day.
> What hours, O what black hours we have we spent
> This night! What sights you, heart, saw; ways you went!
> And more must, in yet longer light's delay.
>   With witness I speak this. But where I say
> Hours I mean years, mean life. And my lament
> Is cries countless, cries like dead letters sent
> To dearest him that lives, alas, away.

>   I am gall, I am heartburn. God's most deep decree
> Bitter would have me taste: my taste was me;
> Bones built in me, flesh filled, blood brimmed the curse.
>   Selfyeast of spirit a dull dough sours. I see
> The lost are like this, and their scourge to be
> As I am mine, their sweating selves; but worse.

Dickinson wrote no sonnets, and Hopkins virtually no poems in short-lined quatrains, but his experiments with sonnet form (breaking up the regular metre with speech-rhythms, adding extra lines) are actually rather similar to her experiments with quatrains. The word-play (is 'fell' a noun – meaning 'mountain' – or an adjective used substantivally?), the unidiomatic sentences that nonetheless have the feel of being idiomatic ('dearest him that lives, alas, away'), the inventive use of metaphor, the speaking voice insisting on not being contradicted ('with witness I speak this') – all these are unmistakeably Hopkins, yet it is so easy to describe them so that they sound like Dickinson.

There are resemblances, too, in subject-matter: happy poems celebrating Nature, and poems of despair about a God who does not answer:

> Of Course – I prayed –
> And did God Care?
> He cared as much as on the Air
> A Bird – had stamped her foot –   (376)

The inescapable difference, of course, is that Hopkins was a Jesuit priest, and his poems of religious despair are written within a framework of orthodoxy: Christian introspection is familiar with the dark night of the soul, in which the self feels abandoned and compares itself to the damned. Orthodoxy knows that this is followed, when God so wills, by the dawn. Yet that dawn gleams with a very faint light in Hopkins' 'terrible sonnets', and in some of them does not gleam at all. Both poets wrote poems in which despair seems to prevail: 'The lost are like this'; 'They no more remember me – / Nor ever turn to tell me why – / Oh, Master, this is misery –'.

As Higginson to Dickinson, so Bridges to Hopkins: each of these two isolated, unpublished, unrecognised poets had a toehold in the conventional literary world. The personal relationship was different: Hopkins and Bridges were friends and equals, whereas Dickinson treated Higginson with deference, calling him 'preceptor', and signing herself 'your scholar'. But for all this deference, she allowed herself to be influenced as little as Hopkins did. For though it was important to both poets to show their poems to somebody, and even to win approval from conventional criticism, it was quite as important to preserve one's independence and refuse to compromise with conventional expectations; and they wrote to their preceptors to say so:

> Obscurity I do and will try to avoid so far as is consistent with excellences higher than clearness at a first reading . . . As for affectation, I do not believe I am guilty of it: you should point out instances, but as long as mere novelty and boldness strikes you as affectation your criticism strikes as – water of the lower Isis.

> I smile when you suggest that I delay 'to publish' – that being foreign to my thought as Firmament to Fin . . . My barefoot Rank is better . . . You think my gait 'spasmodic'. I am in danger, Sir. You think me 'uncon-

trolled'. I have no Tribunal. The sailor cannot see the North, but knows the Needle can.

So similar; and so different. Each is determined to preserve independence, and thus integrity. Hopkins does so in the language of Bridges, with a critical sobriety that uses the terminology of those it is resisting. Dickinson is much more mischievous: she uses her own diction, and her tone is almost impertinent; the result sounds more like one of her own poems than like the solemn doubts of the conservative critic. Just as her withdrawal from society was not bolstered by a counter-tradition like that of the Jesuits, so she sounds more individual, more quirky, and – dare we add? – more feminine.

Note The numbering of the standard edition of Dickinson's poems, edited by Thomas H. Johnson, and published by Little Brown, has become widely accepted, and is used here. Selected letters, also edited by Johnson, are published by the Belknap Press of Harvard: the 'Master' letters are nos 187, 233 and 248. Ransom's remarks on the editing of her poems are in 'Emily Dickinson: a Poet Restored', an essay in *Emily Dickinson: a Collection of Critical Essays,* edited by Richard B. Sewall (1963); Adrienne Rich's reply is in 'Vesuvius at Home: the Power of Dickinson' in *Critical Essays on Emily Dickinson*, ed. Paul Ferlazzo (1984). There is an excellent discussion of the editing of Dickinson by Daniel Karlin in the *London Review of Books* for 24 August 2000. Hopkins' defence of his 'obscurity' is in a letter to Robert Bridges dated 1878 and quoted in the introduction to the Penguin edition of Hopkins' poems, edited by R H Gardner. Dickinson's similar defence is in a letter to Higginson of 7 June 1862.

The Moon's Dropped Child: Charlotte Mew

Fame was one of Charlotte Mew's own favourites among her poems: it displays much of her poetic power, and many of her difficulties.

> Sometimes in the over-heated house, but not for long,
>   Smirking and speaking rather loud,
> I see myself among the crowd,
> Where no-one fits the singer to his song,
> Or sifts the unpainted from the painted faces
> Of the people who are always on my stair;
> They were not with me when I walked in heavenly places;
>   But could I spare

In the blind earth's great silences and spaces,
　　The din, the scuffle, the long stare
　　If I went back and it was not there?
Back to the old known things that are the new,
The folded glory of the gorse, the sweet-briar air,
To the larks that cannot praise us, knowing nothing of what we do
　　And the divine, wise trees that do not care
Yet, to leave Fame, still with such eyes and that bright hair!
God! if I might! And before I go hence
　　Take in her stead
　　To our tossed bed,
One little dream, no matter how small, how wild.
Just now, I think I found it in a field, under a fence –
A frail, dead, new-born lamb, ghostly and pitiful and white,
　　A blot upon the night,
　　The moon's dropped child!

The opening image for fame is a crowd 'of the people who are always on my stair': coarse, invasive, undiscriminating (they do not sift the unpainted from the painted faces), and it is contrasted with the 'heavenly places', where, presumably, she lives with her poems but values them for themselves alone, not for the fame they bring. The contrast is plain enough, but her attitude to it changes, as she thinks about 'the old known things' that the poems are about, but wonders if she could do without the fame they might bring. Perhaps she might, if she could find something to replace it, and the poem ends on an image for what that something might be, the image of the lamb that is never explained but provides the haunting line that concludes the poem.

Like so many of her poems, it has a general argument that is not difficult to make out, but fitting all the details to that can be puzzling. The beautiful list of images listing what the earth offers, and insisting on its indifference to us ('the divine wise trees that do not care') is presumably an account of writing poetry while remaining indifferent to fame (though it is of course such poems that would bring fame). But what of the ending? What is the 'tossed bed' doing there? Until then, the poet has been an individual, but now suddenly she is part of a couple ('*our* tossed bed'). And though the image of the dead lamb is hauntingly beautiful, what is its place in the argument? Does it represent a dream that is too private to write about, a renunciation of poetry? The argument of this poem is not obscure, but its most moving details are those which are hard to fit into that argument.

The poem is certainly not part of an autobiography. Mew never achieved much in the way of fame and died obscure (though she did win the praises of Thomas Hardy and the support of Harold Monro and the Poetry bookshop); and she may never have shared her 'tossed bed' with anyone (she was lesbian in her sexual orientation, but quite possibly never a practising one).

Mew's contact with the modernist movement was minimal: she published anywhere that would take her writing, and this brought a passing contact with the editors of *The Yellow Book* and even with Ezra Pound, but she seems to have had no interest in movements and theories: if there is anything modernist about her poetry, it is simply the result of her pursuing her own vision and way of writing. A short poem called *The Call* tells how 'we' sat by the fire and heard a strange call which could not be resisted:

> Something swift and tall
> Swept in and out and that was all.
> Was it a bright or a dark angel? Who can know?

This is not the incomprehensibility of modernism, it is the mysteriousness of many late Victorian poets encountering the strange and the supernatural. Yet though Mew did not set out to write poetry in a new way, her poems do seem to belong in the 20th century, leaving unanswered not only questions about their subject-matter, but about the way they are organised. *The Forest Road*, for instance, one of her strangest and most haunting poems, seems to be an account of some loved person (almost certainly a woman) on the edge of madness or a breakdown, but not only are we told nothing of the circumstances, we also do not know the sex of the speaker.

> What is this singing on the road
> That makes all other music like the music in a dream?

Is this more like the haunting music of a Victorian – Tennyson, say, or Sidney Dobell – or the nightmare music of *The Waste Land*? Perhaps there is no need to decide that: classifying poets into schools, identifying modernism, has its uses but can obscure the continuities of poetic practice.

Mew's fascination with madness is implicit in many of her poems, and also quite explicit in some. Sometimes, as in *Ken*, the speaker is wholly sane and just moved by pity:

Nothing was dead:
 He said 'a bird' if he picked up a broken wing,
A perished leaf or any such thing
Was just 'a rose' . . .

More often, a touch of strangeness seems to have crept into the writing of the poem. And in *The Farmer's Bride,* her most famous poem – the one most likely to be familiar to those who know nothing about her – the speaker is wholly sane, indeed ordinary:

Three summers since I chose a maid,
  Too young maybe – but more's to do
At harvest time than bide and woo.
  When us was wed she turned afraid
Of love and me and all things human.

The speaker of *The Farmer's Bride* clearly does not understand the strange woman he has married: all he can suggest is that she was 'too young'. He tells how she ran away, was caught, and locked in the house. Now she does her housework 'as long as men-folk keep away'. He is tormented, first by the absence of children at Christmas time, then by his own frustrated sexual desire:

She sleeps up in the attic there
  Alone, poor maid. 'Tis but a stair
Betwixt us. Oh! My God! the down
  The soft young down of her, the brown,
The brown of her – her eyes, her hair! Her hair!

The inarticulate speaker is an unavoidable problem for the writer of a dramatic monologue: can the strange quality of the young wife's neurosis be conveyed by someone who so clearly does not understand it? It is a problem but also an advantage, since nobody really understands such a woman, and his puzzled pity, though not the only way to write about 'her wild self', invites the reader to share the puzzlement. This choice of a perfectly ordinary narrator is the main objection that some have had to the poem. H. W. Nevinson, reviewing the volume when it appeared in 1916, complained : 'A man can hardly imagine why the most sensitive of women should run out into the night to avoid him.' Feminist critics are used to the coarse male generalisation that knows what 'a woman' can and can't feel; here, interestingly, the coarseness is reversed: it is 'a man' who is generalised into a monolithic example of his sex.

Perhaps none of Mew's poems is so immediately clear and yet so puzzling if we try to interpret it as *A Quoi Bon Dire*.

> Seventeen years ago you said
>   Something that sounded like Good-bye;
>   And everybody thinks that you are dead,
>   But I.
>
>   So I, as I grow stiff and cold
>   To this and that say Good-bye too;
>   And everybody thinks that I am old
>   But you.
>
>   And one fine morning in a sunny lane
>   Some boy and girl will meet and kiss and swear
>   That nobody can love their way again
>   While over there
>   You will have smiled, I shall have tossed your hair.

Right from the title, this teases the reader: does the title allude to the poem from without, asking what is the use of recalling such an episode, such a memory? Or should we think of it as a remark made within the poem: what is the use of the speaker remembering what happened seventeen years ago? And who is dead, who alive? The speaker seems to be alive, though old; but what of the 'you'? Above all, where is 'over there': the land of the living, seen by the dead, or the land of the dead, seen by the living, or nothing so straightforward as either of these? I have read several discussions of this poem, and they seem to make no attempt to answer these questions – and perhaps they are right not to. Even to put such straightforward questions to a poem like this is to tear the heart out of its mystery – yet does it not insist on such questions? With none of the theorising, none of the vocabulary, of modernism Mew seems to have written a truly modernist poem.

4

The Twentieth Century

Ecriture Féminine and Modernism: A Note

Now, despite the disclaimer in the Introduction, a touch of literary theory: brief, and (I hope) useful for introducing the moderns – or some of them. *Ecriture féminine* sounds relevant to a discussion of women's writing – or at least modern women's writing: is it?

The term implies a claim that women's language can (and should) avoid the masculinist bias that is so strong in ordinary language: should reject convention and rationality, should 'write the body'. Its favourite terms for what should be rejected in language, besides 'convention' and 'rationality' are 'masculinist thinking' and also (a term which indicates its strongly psycho-analytic strain) 'phallocentrism'. Thus Hélène Cixous writes:

> Nearly the entire history of writing is confounded with the history of reason, of which it is at once the effect, the support, and one of the privileged alibis. It has been one with the phallocentric tradition. It is indeed that same self-admiring, self-stimulating, self-congratulatory phallocentrism.

And Mary Daly claims that 'gynocentric experience means risking', and describes her writing practice thus: 'Since the language and style of patriarchal writing simply cannot contain or carry the energy of women's exorcism and ecstasy, in this book I invent, dis-cover, re-member.'

There are clear resemblances between this programme and the modernist programme in poetry, first formulated by Mallarmé and Valéry in France, then by Eliot and Pound in England and America. Valéry aspired to a poetry that could never be reduced to the expression of a thought, that could never be translated into other terms without perishing; and Mallarmé gave the following memorable description of poetic language:

The verse which out of several word-units refashions a single word, new, foreign to the language, incantatory as it were, consummates this isolation of the verbal element: denying, by one sovereign stroke, the element of chance which remains in the words we use despite the process of their alternate immersion in sense and sound, and causing us the shock of never having heard this particular ordinary fragment of elocution, at the same time as our memory of the thing named is bathed in a transfiguring light.

In much the same spirit, Eliot urged the modern poet 'to force, to dislocate if necessary, language into his meaning', and Pound, more brutally, commanded: 'Make it new'.

'Je suis là où ça parle.' I am there where it speaks: 'it' could be the unconscious/ the female unconscious/ the Freudian id – or should be left unspecified. This short sentence by Hélène Cixous epitomises the linguistic radicalism of *écriture féminine*, and shows its similarity with some of the most extreme forms of literary modernism. But there is one striking and important difference. Valéry and Mallarmé, Eliot and Pound, contrasted their modernist programme with other, more familiar and straightforward uses of language: Valéry envied the musician the fact that he left the world of noise for that of sound, and felt that the modern poet should search for a corresponding way of constructing 'a language within the language'. He compared the language of poetry to dancing, and ordinary language to walking. *Ecriture féminine,* on the other hand usually seems to claim that *all* your language, if you are a woman, should aim to 'write your self', should give you back your 'immense bodily territories which have been kept under seal.' All language? What then of the directions that to find the headquarters of the women's co-operative you take the second turning on the right, look for no. 17 and go up to the third floor? That is not – and could not be – in a form of language that realises the decensored relation of woman to her sexuality: if we are to find the place we're looking for, we need ordinary rational, 'phallocentric' language. The fact that theories of *écriture féminine* do not trouble to mention this point could simply be because it is so obvious, so that only the male aiming to score points would bother to mention it, if it were not for one thing: what of women scientists? Science is necessarily in the language of rationality, in a language that uses the 'ready made grids' denounced by Irigary, Cixous and Kristeva; and if the theory of *écriture féminine* leads to an attack on female scientists as having sold out to phallocentrism, then it finds itself allied to the most reactionary form of male chauvinism: the assertion that women are not really capable of becoming scientists, because rationalist thinking is too much for them.

We can make this correction, and consider the theory of *écriture fémi-nine* as an account of one kind of language – important, but not the only important kind. It then becomes not a theory about language, not even a theory about poetry, but a theory about modernist poetry. And then when we look for the modern poems that it describes, we find that they are mostly by men: by Pound and Eliot, by Mallarmé and Rimbaud,. by Benn and Stevens. Perhaps we should designate these men as honorary women. Plenty of women, after all, achieving distinction in traditionally male fields, have been treated as honorary men If we must categorise, it might be time for a change.

The Americans

Modernism bit deeper into American poetry than it did into English; and the best and most interesting women poets of the early and mid 20th century were Americans. There may be no connection between these two assertions, though the convinced modernist will, of course, see them as cause and effect. The seven poets discussed in this chapter had very different relations to modernism, and I shall not try to see them as consti-tuting a single phenomenon, except to say that they are, arguably, the best women poets of the 20th century.

Marianne Moore

If there is any poet whom one wants to approach through her critics it is surely the scholarly, eccentric and often inaccessible Marianne Moore; and if there is any poet whose critics are eccentric, inaccessible and (often) pleased with themselves, it is certainly Marianne Moore. So where should one start?

It is best to start with a poem, and preferably with one that is typical, much admired, and full of her characteristic difficulties: and so I will start with *The Pangolin*. This poem is full of – indeed, is built on – what Randall Jarrell accurately calls her 'almost ostentatious lack of transitions and explanations' . The reader needs confidence that, after it has been read over and over, a paraphraseable meaning will emerge, and it even-tually does – more or less. After five stanzas about this oddly shaped ant-eater and its behaviour, full of meticulous descriptive details (it has a peculiar step 'that the outside / edges of its hands may bear the weight and save the claws / for digging'), the subject then changes to 'man', who shares with the pangolin the quaint distinction of being a mammal ('warm blood, no gills, two pairs of hands and a few hairs'). Mankind is in some ways less efficient than the pangolin ('the prey of fear, . . . thwarted by the dusk') but has a degree of consciousness celebrated in the poem's splendid concluding lines, in which man says to 'alternating blaze':

> 'Again the sun!
> anew each day; and new and new and new,
> that comes into and steadies my soul.'

But in order to confront the full difficulty of reading Moore, we need to read slowly and meticulously, and perhaps the best way to do this is to look carefully at a single stanza. I have chosen the sixth. After the lovingly precise description of the pangolin and its habits, its 'sting-proof scales; and nest / of rocks closed with earth from inside, which he can thus darken' this stanza begins the transition from the pangolin itself to the parallels it offers for the human situation. .

We have just been told that the pangolin is 'made graceful by adversities'; after that, stanza 6 offers an exploration of the various meanings of 'grace'.

> versities.　To explain grace requires
> 　a curious hand.　If that which is at all were not forever,
> why would those who graced the spires
> with animals and gathered there to rest, on cold luxurious
> low stone seats – a monk and monk and monk – between the thus
> 　ingenious roof supports, have slaved to confuse
> 　　grace with a kindly manner, time in which to pay a debt,
> 　the cure for sins, a graceful use
> 　　of what are yet
> 　　　approved stone mullions branching out across
> 　　　the perpendiculars? A sailboat

Two stanzas then speak about human beings, and a final stanza – teasingly – begins by leaving us wondering whether it is about man or the pangolin, but in the end is clearly in praise of man – and Moore, never politically correct, has no hesitation in saying 'man' when she means 'humanity'.

What is this 6th stanza saying? Among other things, it is a kind of dictionary entry of the various meanings of 'grace': 'a kindly manner', as in 'the grace he shows in his way of greeting'; 'time in which to pay a debt' as in 'You have a grace period of one month before the policy lapses'; the theological meaning ('a cure for sins'); and the pleasing elegance of architectural decoration (the grace of these stone mullions). But it is also a declaration of Christian faith: if there were no immortal life, why would the monks (sitting next to each other on the stone bench) have 'graced' their church with sculpture? This is what I take the lines to be saying, but I confess I am puzzled by the use of 'confuse'. In what is surely a Christian poem (and is so read by its many admiring critics), the various secular meanings of 'grace' need to be *distinguished from,* not confused with, the religious meaning, which would be the one that mattered to the monks. By slightly straining the meaning we could read the line as saying that the monks strained [only for us] to confuse, but to me this sounds clumsy. That is a puzzle which no critic I have read is able to explain – or even to notice. A different kind of problem is presented by the argument of the stanza: it is clearly claiming that the work of the Christian sculptors would not have been worth doing 'if that which is at all were not forever'. This is a religious explanation of the beauty of church architecture and decoration, which the monks themselves would have given: but it is also a claim that non-Christians have denied, often vehemently. Those who do not believe in an afterlife are rightly indignant when told that their scepticism makes it pointless to create anything beautiful. Is that what Moore is here maintaining? It seems to be, and she herself seems to have held orthodox Christian beliefs: a poem like this will therefore require the secular reader to read it as he or she reads Donne or Herbert or Milton, but the many secular critics of this poem seem to show no hesitation in accepting its argument.

When Moore writes about the many animals or plants that fascinate her (especially, one might note, the armoured ones), she makes it clear that she is interested in them for themselves, rather than as metaphors for humanity, yet she often does use them as metaphors for humanity as well – for poets, after all, love to have their cake and eat it; and none more so than Marianne Moore.

And what of the form of this poem? Is it in free verse, which Moore often uses and almost always appears to use? The reader will no doubt have noticed that the stanza already quoted ends with what looks like the beginning of a new sentence and begins with the end of a word (the previous stanza ended with 'con –'). This is a by-product of Moore's syllabics. Instead of a regular pattern of stressed and unstressed syllables, as is normal in English verse, her lines, ignoring this difference, attend to the number of syllables in the line, whether stressed or unstressed. To discover this pattern it is necessary to count syllables; here is the result:

Stanza 1: 9,14,9,17,11,11,15,8,5,9,9.
Stanza 2: 9,15,8,16,13,13,13,8,4,10,10.
Stanza 3: 8,14,9,16,13,11,14,11,5,9,9.

Each line differs from the corresponding line in another stanza either not at all or by one or at most two syllables: not quite but very nearly a regular pattern. Whereas regular metre is immediately clear to the reader (even more, to the listener), it is not at all certain whether a reader will notice this pattern, though he may, if he gets to know the poem well, get a feel that there is some kind of regularity somewhere.

As with metre, so with rhyme. First, a general note about rhyme. There are two arguments for rhyme, one focused on the reader, one on the writer. For the reader, rhyme can bring pleasure, both the delight of the familiar and the shock of the unexpected. Thus Anne Finch, longing for an 'absolute retreat', decides that she would like to share it with a man:

> Give me there (since heaven has shown
> It was not good to be alone)
> A partner suited to my mind,
> Solitary, pleased and kind.

The rhymes have an inevitability that seems to correspond to the inevitability of needing a companion. It was the Book of Genesis that said it was not good for Adam to be alone, and the tidiness of the rhyme sends a kind of nod of acknowledgement to the authority; as if, when the partner really suits her mind, his qualities will show their fittingness by rhyming. This satisfying competence required no great originality on the part of the poet, who is simply making fitting use of established practice. But when Macbeth, after agonising over his intended murder of Duncan in agonised blank verse rhythms, hears the bell that tells him everything is ready to kill Duncan, he breaks out into

> Hear it not Duncan, for it is a knell
> That summons thee to heaven – or to Hell!

This time we did not expect rhyme, so it drags us back into a conventional morality that Macbeth's deeply personal soliloquising had somehow forgotten about, yet always knew was there. God's justice is always there, though behind the scenes: as the conventional expectation of rhyme in poetry is always lurking.

For Marianne Moore the expected is always there, always lurking, but the poem strives to avoid it. So her procedure with rhyme is, often, to use it but pretend she hasn't: the rhymes are there but they are concealed from our notice. *Nevertheless* is an interesting example. This is a poem about plants, and particularly about their sometimes astonishing ability to survive in hostile conditions: the poet saw a prickly-pear leaf clinging to barbed wire, the plant flowered because

> a root shot down to grow
> in earth two feet below;

– and the poem is filled with other, similar examples. Typically for Moore, the poem takes an adverb for its title, as if a title like *Survival* or *Persistence* would be too moralistic. Yet she is prepared, right at the end, to moralise:

> What is there

> like fortitude! What sap
> went through that little thread
> to make the cherry red!

– and the poem, which has so far used typically Moore-like unobtrusive rhymes ('multitude/food', 'under/stir'), ends, as it boasts of the prominent colour of the fruit, by flaunting its most prominent rhyme – as if the plant is saying 'I too have something to boast about.'

Back now to *The Pangolin*. Most hearers of this poem would assume that it is unrhymed, but this is not so: the rhyme scheme of the stanza quoted above is *abaccdedefg:* the other stanzas have a similar but not identical pattern. (It is difficult to be certain about the rhyme scheme, since Moore allows herself some very approximate rhymes: I have included in the count some endings that are similar but not the same (*luxurious / thus*), and by including others that are further apart (*yet / sailboat*) I could have claimed even more rhymes. Other stanzas contain a similar but not identical pattern. Once again, the poet has offered us patterning that varies slightly but, once you begin to notice it, is unmistakeably there (the general intention seems to be to have more rhymes at the beginning than the end of each stanza.)

What is the point of this? Rhyme and metre are effects perceived by and giving pleasure to the reader: to the poet, they will be a labour (delightful to some poets, burdensome to others). In Marianne Moore the purpose seems to be the opposite: they are there to give the burden to the poet without necessarily being perceived by the reader. It is virtually a way of saying to the reader: I have taken trouble, which was no doubt good for me, whether you are aware of it or not.

But to say this one needs a reader who *is* aware of it, and this is ensured by a detail that must strike anyone reading this stanza: that it begins in the middle of a word. By quoting the stanza out of its context I made the first line seem even odder than it is: when we read it as part of the poem, we see that 'versities' is the ending of 'conversities'. Splitting the word has helped to preserve the syllable-count, and has also (perhaps: I am not sure of this) offered a possible (though hardly noticeable) rhyme between 'con' and 'done' four lines earlier. The poet appears to be telling the reader: 'Yes, this is odd; but when I set myself a rule – as one does in syllabics, though it may not be noticed – I stick to it.'

No Swan so Fine is one of her most anthologised poems, though it is by means straightforward.

> 'No water so still as the
>   dead fountains of Versailles.' No swan,
> with swart blind look askance
> and gondoliering legs, so fine
>   as the chintz china one with fawn-
> brown eyes and toothed gold
> collar on to show whose bird it was.
>
> Lodged in the Louis Fifteenth
>   candelabrum-tree of cockscomb-
> tinted buttons, dahlias,
> sea urchins, and everlastings,
>   it perches on the branching foam
> of polished sculptured
> flowers – at ease and tall. The king is dead.

Is this Moore's version of the *Ode on a Grecian Urn* or *Sailing to Byzantium*, those wonderful poems about the superiority of art to nature? Keats and Yeats celebrate art because, though it does not move and breathe, it captures the vitality of life better than any merely natural object; *No Swan so Fine,* however seems to invite us to rejoice in the artificiality itself, as if the beauty of art resides in its being *unlike* life. The real swan looks askance and uses its legs like an artificially twisted oar, the 'chintz china' swan stands 'at ease and tall'. And what is the point of that last, brief sentence? That the king, who ordered the swan to be made, is dead but the swan lives on? Or is everything dead in Versailles – beautiful but dead – and the swan's function is to remind us of this? Moore is not always averse to drawing a moral, but the moral of her poems is often ambivalent, sometimes even unclear.

Moore stated something like her own creed in *Poetry*, with its arresting opening: 'I too dislike it: there are things that are important beyond all this fiddle.' In itself, that could be an aggressively philistine statement, a way of preferring life to art, especially to pernickety, over-elaborated art (like that chintz china swan), but what exactly a Moore poem is maintaining will seldom stand still enough to be inspected, and we hardly need to remind ourselves that if Moore dislikes poetry it is only in the way poetry-lovers and poets 'dislike' it. She makes her position clearer when she quotes Tolstoi (she is always quoting somebody, in her poems), who claimed that poetry is 'everything with the exception of business documents and schoolbooks'; Moore replies 'nor is it valid to discriminate against "business documents and schoolbooks".' So is she adopting the strategy of telling us what poetry is not, and then claiming that it could be that too? Then, not exactly as a definition, rather as an exhortation addressed to the poets, she adds, in what has become the most famous phrase she ever wrote, that poems have 'imaginary gardens with real toads in them'. Moore's admirers seldom pause to explain this wonderful image: is it saying that the descriptions are imaginary, the emotions real? or that the pretty bits are imaginary, the ugly parts real? or that the conventional descriptions are imaginary, the original touches real? Well, poems should no more be paraphrased than the tomb of Longfellow visited.

Marianne Moore – there is no getting away from it – is a difficult poet; and having begun with one difficult poem, I shall now look at *Marriage*: the longest and perhaps the strangest poem she ever wrote. It begins with a thoughtful comment on the nature of marriage:

> This institution,
> perhaps one should say enterprise
> out of respect for which
> one says one need not change one's mind
> about a thing one has believed in,
> requiring public promises
> of one's intention
> to fulfil a private obligation.

This is the most direct attempt in the whole poem to make a statement about marriage, and the statement is a paradox. Is that a sign of the absurdity of making marriage an institution, or of the necessary paradox of human institutions? We soon realise that we are not to expect answers. That so flamboyant a spinster should dare to write this poem is an act both bold and oblique – as is the poem. Much of it consists of collage: the juxtaposition of quotations from very varied sources, with no explanations or sources given: a method that critics have compared to Dadaism, to the paintings of Marcel Duchamp or to Eliot's *The Waste Land;* and academic critics have meticulously traced these sources. I will take one brief example. Adam and Eve, since they are the oldest married couple, appear frequently and fitfully in the poem ('I wonder what Adam and Eve / think of it by this time'), and after one of the mentions of Adam come the lines:

> "something feline,
> something colubrine" – how true!

It is not even clear, in the telegraphic style of this poem, that these words apply to Adam, but critics have, probably rightly, assumed that they do. Why is Adam like a cat and like a snake? Is it meant to connect with the mention of the serpent, only six lines earlier, as 'that invaluable accident / exonerating Adam'? Is it a suggestion that Adam himself was, or could be seen as, the serpent? The fact that these four words are in quotation marks clearly indicates that they are a quotation, and a note by Moore provides us with the source: they come from a review of George Santayana's *Poems* in *The New Republic.* They were not, that is, about Adam at all, but have been applied to him by the poem, so that 'how true' is in a sense misleading, since it looks like, but isn't, a nod of assent to what the words originally meant. The four words are fascinating: what reminds us both of a cat and of a snake? They seem to me more likely to apply to the style of a poem than to Adam, but we look in vain in the poem for an explanation of why they have been transferred in this way.

Moore herself made no secret of her pilfering of quotations from widely differing sources, and described them as 'statements which took my fancy which I tried to arrange plausibly'. Plausibly? Does that mean that they are about, or can be applied to, marriage? Some are; others seem to be wrenched almost arbitrarily from their original context. The poem ends with a reference to the American statesman Daniel Webster, a quotation from the inscription on his statue, and a description of him (or of a wedding ceremony?) – 'the Book on the writing table; / the hand in the breast pocket' – which may or may not be intended as mockery.

May or may not: the many commentators on this poem differ in what they consider is ironic and what isn't. They differ less in their readiness to praise the poem, not only for its ironies but for 'its use of random syllabics'. Certainly the poem uses neither traditional metre nor the often very strict syllabic patterns she sometimes imposes on her work. But what are 'random syllabics', one wonders: are they any different from simple randomness? *Marriage* is the longest of Moore's poems, in some ways the most ambitious, but also the most eccentric; it is also, perhaps, the one most likely to divide her more sceptical admirers from those who like her best when she is most random.

It seems unkind to end what for many may be a first introduction to Moore with her most difficult, most enigmatic poem; so I will conclude with her simplest, which is also, perhaps, her most anthologised.

Silence

My father used to say,
'Superior people never make long visits,
have to be shown Longfellow's grave
or the glass flowers at Harvard.
Self-reliant like the cat –
That takes its prey to privacy,
The mouse's limp tail hanging like a shoelace from its mouth –
They sometimes enjoy solitude,
And can be robbed of speech
By speech which has delighted them.
The deepest feeling always shows itself in silence;
Not in silence, but restraint.'
Nor was he insincere in saying, 'Make my house your inn.'
Inns are not residences.

The only possible puzzle with this poem is whether or not the poet's attitude to her father is ironic: is she passing on his words of wisdom, or allowing him to betray his limited or pompous opinions? If we turn to the poet's biography we'll discover that her father abandoned his family, and so treated his own house as an inn, not a residence, but the poem is not, of course, written for those who know this: Moore is not a poet who talks about her own personal life. The content of what her father used to say is not only attractive in itself, but seems to express a view of life that the poet, to judge from her other work, found sympathetic: she loved watching and noting details of animal behaviour (indeed, this is the most striking quality of her poems), she loved precise, even fussy verbal discriminations, often expressed as self-correction, like 'shows itself in silence; Not in silence, but restraint.' Being robbed of speech by speech which has delighted you has the ring of many of Moore's aphorisms. Perhaps 'superior' is a bit odd: not quite the term we'd expect such a thoughtful, discriminating person to use: we can all too easily imagine the visitor to Longfellow's grave remarking that he was a *superior* poet. So is Marianne Moore teasing us? All too likely, perhaps. Is the reader's limp tail hanging from the poem's mouth?

Note   Marianne Moore's poems are widely reprinted and anthologised: the most convenient British edition is that of Faber and Faber (1968); because she so often revised and abridged her poems, however, this edition, which prints the latest versions, reduces her most famous poem, *Poetry*, to three rather trite lines. There are abundant – and lengthy – discussions of her poems on the internet; of the many published essays on her work, that of Randall Jarrell (in his *Poetry & the Age)* is especially attractive and enthusiastic.

Elizabeth Bishop

Elizabeth Bishop was an admirer and friend of Marianne Moore, and wrote a poem about her:

> From Brooklyn, over the Brooklyn Bridge, on this fine morning,
>   please come flying.
> In a cloud of fiery pale chemicals,
>   please come flying . . .
>
> Come with the pointed toe of each black shoe
> trailing a sapphire highlight,
> with a black capeful of butterfly wings and bon-mots,
> with heaven knows how many angels all riding
> on the broad black brim of your hat,
>   please come flying . . .

This is a charming but utterly misleading poem. The details about Moore's personal appearance and habits (the shoes, the cape, the hat) may be accurate, but the suggestion that Moore was a poet of whimsy, of impudent fancy, is quite wrong. Bishop was convinced that as a poet she owed more to Moore than to anyone, yet it is understandable that critics should consider this her worst poem. We need to find somewhere else to begin, so let us rather begin with the first poem in her *Complete Poems*. It is called 'The Map':

> Labrador's yellow, where the moony Eskimo
> Has oiled it . . . .
> The names of seashore towns run out to sea,
> The names of cities cross the neighbouring mountains . . .
> These peninsulas take the water between thumb and finger
> Like women feeling for the smoothness of yard-goods.

Most people have not been to Labrador; and even those who have, looking at it on a map, experience an act of representation, not a recapturing of what it was like to be there; so a poem about a map might as well accept this, and enjoy, not the experience of being there, but the act of representing. We know perfectly well that Labrador isn't actually yellow, so the map-maker's arbitrary choice of colours can be seen as a game (where the rules are arbitrary) and an opportunity to invent explanations of our own that are obviously wrong but are fun. We know perfectly well that nothing runs out into the real sea or crosses the real mountains, but a map appears to pretend that it does.

To call this a structuralist poem is both correct and absurdly wrong: It is about the nature of representation, as is structuralism; but it treats this not as the basis of a theory, but as fun. The simile in those last two lines is brilliantly wrong: the peninsulas are not *doing* anything, as the women are, so the comparison is being imposed by the poet's game of pretending that they are. She is joking, but she is also noticing.

Turn on a few pages, and we find a poem called 'Wading at Wellfleet', built on the observation that the coldness of the sea is like a case of knives: it tells us that the ancient Assyrians invented a chariot 'that bore sharp blades around its wheels', and it begins to explore the parallel (when we stand in the cold sea, the spokes are 'directed at the shin'). The parallel in this poem is a bit less arbitrary, but it breaks down as we read:

> The war rests wholly with the waves:
> They try revolving, but the wheels
> Give way; they will not bear the weight.

Comparisons never can be maintained, if we ask too much of them, but all the same they are the lifeblood of poetry: this comparison is kept up for most of the poem, then dropped. This is a poet who understands structuralist theory, though she does not theorise: she writes poems.

Turn a few more pages and we find 'Questions of Travel', which is about real places, not their representation on maps, so that

> the mountains look like the hulls of capsized ships,
> slime-hung and barnacled

– a brilliant image, though more conventional in its functioning, since it offers an actual visual resemblance between the two items. This poem is about our modern passion for travel, which is first of all wittily questioned, asking what childishness leads us

>   to rush
> to see the sun the other way round.

The poem does not bother to point out that this piece of geographical knowledge, acquired from books, is not confirmed when we actually travel and find that the sun looks just the same. Elizabeth Bishop did more than her fair share of travelling, and actually lived in Brazil for 15 years, so the poem naturally goes on to make the case that travel does after all enrich our experience, by listing a few things it would have been a pity to miss. They are not the sights and experiences set out in the travel brochures, but (as one might expect from a poet) the small, ordinary experiences of seeing particular trees, of hearing 'the fat brown bird . . . in a bamboo church of Jesuit baroque' or of hearing

> The sad, two-noted, wooden tune
> Of disparate wooden clogs
> Carelessly clacking over
> A grease-stained filling-station floor.

Ordinariness is individual in Brazil, and to drive the point home the poem adds:

> In another country the clogs would all be tested.
> Each pair there would have identical pitch.

(the 'other country' is presumably the United States, where things are made in factories and therefore uniform. Since the poem is about – and in praise of – travel, it is worth wondering about the Brazilian who travels to the United States, from the disparate wooden clogs to the uniformity of the mass-produced: is he too enriched?)

Bishop is not afraid to write descriptive poems. I say 'not afraid', because a descriptive poem is a way of resting on the poet's confidence in her own talent. It does not announce a subject heavy with significance, it does not impose the poet's vision on the observable world, it simply enjoys the process of observing and finding verbal equivalents for the world. We can take *At the Fishhouses* as an example. The title announces that no preconceived significance is being imposed on the subject, and this does indeed turn out to be the case: the poem moves like a leisurely stroll among the fishhouses, noting the interesting people she meets, the interesting reflections they suggest.

> The air smells so strongly of codfish
> It makes one's nose run and one's eyes water.

Correct, and unmemorable: but what, we can ask, gives the poem more interest than the stroll which the poet took? There is, in the first place, the wit: 'one seal particularly' was there evening after evening:

> He was curious about me. He was interested in music;
> Like me a believer in total immersion.

The only reason for claiming that the seal was 'interested in music' is of course that the poet sang to him and he did not go away: it's a way of pretending – and of enjoying the pretence. There is no reason to believe that the real Elizabeth Bishop was a Baptist who believed in total immersion rather than the mere symbolic wetting that Anglicans perform: it is simply an opportunity for her wit.

Then, continuing her walk, she notices the forest of 'dignified tall firs', and responds to the fact that they are grown by us for our own purposes:

> A million Christmas trees stand
> waiting for Christmas.

If waiting is a conscious process (as it would be with us) this is a joke; if waiting simply means that they'll be there until they are cut down, it's a literal statement.

Then, at the end, the poem grows more ambitious: having been so conscientiously descriptive, it now offers a reflection that could be called philosophical. The water, it concludes,

. . . is like what we imagine knowledge to be:
dark, salt, clear, moving utterly free,
drawn from the cold hard mouth
of the world, derived from the rocky breasts
forever . . .

This is so suggestive that any paraphrase would oversimplify, but one thing is clear: it tells us that knowledge comes from outside ourselves. The scientist and the religious reader, though for different reasons, can assent to this, and a poem in which the poet seemed completely in control of what was said concludes in humility: knowledge comes to us from the world, and is a mystery. Just as Elizabeth Bishop's poems come from outside herself.

In order to look at a whole poem, I have chosen *One Art*.

The art of losing isn't hard to master;
so many things seem filled with the intent
to be lost that their loss is no disaster.

Lose something every day. Accept the fluster
of lost door keys, the hour badly spent.
The art of losing isn't hard to master.

Then practise losing farther, losing faster:
places, and names, and where it was you meant
to travel. None of these will bring disaster.

I lost my mother's watch. And look! My last, or
next to last, of three loved houses, went.
The art of losing isn't hard to master.

I lost two cities, lovely ones. And, vaster,
some realms I owned, two rivers, a continent.
I miss them, but it wasn't a disaster.

– Even losing you (the joking voice, a gesture
I love) I shan't have lied. It's evident
the art of losing's not too hard to master
though it may look like (*Write* it!) like disaster.

The villanelle is a form devised in 16th century France, where is was used mainly for pastoral songs; it was revived in late 19th century England for light verse. William Empson, followed by Auden and Dylan Thomas, was mainly responsible for introducing it into modern English as a form for serious poetry, and as with all successful steps in technique it now seems astonishing that earlier poets had not realised its serious power. Its mounting repetitions, its generalising force, and the firmness with which its conclusion refuses to say anything new, all add to the authority that a well written villanelle can impose on its assertions. No important poet has written more than one or two villanelles (this is the only one in Bishop's *Complete Poems),* and its impact tends to be so general that more than one or two would easily lead to an impression of repetition, and undermine the authoritative feel.

Losing something can be trivial or serious, depending not only on what is lost but on how we regarded it; and the injunction 'lose something every day' can be light-hearted or very serious. Or it can be a light-hearted, injunction, jokey in tone, that we are then invited to take seriously. It is obvious that the objects lost in the course of this poem grow more and more serious as it proceeds, and this means that the repeated assertion that the loss is 'no disaster' grows more and more desperate, less and less convincing. The most important loss is of 'you' in the final stanza: we're told this by the opening word, 'even', and by the personal details in parenthesis, and this prepares us for the possibility that this is the loss that *does* matter, that we cannot shrug off by not caring about it, as in the first five stanzas. The end of the poem, therefore, could be the moment when we are finally told that it was whistling in the dark to keep its spirits up; but we are only told this in a subordinate clause, a modification, at most, of the repeated assertions that have clanged through the poem:

Though it may look like (*Write* it!) like disaster.

Anne Stevenson reads the ending of the poem very differently. 'Losing,' she claims, 'is an "art" indispensable to the art of writing': she then quotes the last two lines, and adds her interpretation: ' "write it" asks, too, to be read as 'right it'; to write something is to right it. Thus a poem begun in despair became . . . a poem about the triumph of poetry.'

It is not uncommon for critics to leap on the moments when a poem can be read as being about its own writing. Some poems are; but the critic, especially the modernist critic, for whom the nature of poetry is a central concern, is too often tempted to see a poem in this way. As, I believe, Stevenson was tempted: not only do I find her reading mistaken, it also seems to me to diminish the poem. 'Write it' does not, except to the over-sophisticated commentator, 'ask' to be read as 'right it', and the painful truth that so many poems teach us is that writing does not 'right' things. To me the italics in the last line are saying 'admit it': put down the painful truth that the poem has avoided until this last moment, the truth that though we may dismiss (or pretend to dismiss) other losses as trivial, 'losing you' really would be a disaster. Compared with this deeply tragic reading, the sophisticated pun which Stevenson finds is superficial.

To approach a poem through a disagreement with another critic may seem very academic, even Alexandrian, but I have done it here because I wish to defend the power of the poem against a misreading that trivialises it, turning into a piece of literary theory what was offered as a painful confession.

Note   Elizabeth Bishop's *Complete Poems* are published by Chatto & Windus (2004). Anne Stevenson's discussion of *One Art* is in her book *Elizabeth Bishop* (1966), which is also a valuable biographical study.

Two Retellings: H.D. & Denise Levertov

Poets have always liked to retell old stories. Even when they try to be faithful to the original version, some trace of the new poet's age or allegiances is likely to appear; sometimes this is the express purpose of the retelling.

The figure of Orpheus has probably haunted later poetry as much as any other: he represents the magical power of poetry and of music, which could charm animals and even trees, which 'bowed themselves when he did sing'. When his wife Eurydice, fleeing from a ravisher, trod on a snake and died, Orpheus followed her into the underworld in order to win her back; his song so ravished the dark gods that she was allowed to follow him back to earth – but on condition that he did not look back until they returned to the light. He reached the upper air and in his eagerness turned back before she had joined him; whereupon she vanished and he lost her. He met his death by being torn to pieces by the Maenads, women intoxicated with the worship of Bacchus.

Two women poets of the 20th century have retold this story. H.D. (Hilda Doolittle was always known by her initials) chose to tell the story of the failed rescue of Eurydice, and Denise Levertov chose to tell of the magical power of his poetry.

The tragic failure of the rescue of Eurydice has always been interpreted as showing the overeagerness of love, perhaps along with the way a command of the gods could be a trap if not followed meticulously. But this is not how H.D.'s Eurydice sees it:

> so for your arrogance
> and your ruthlessness
> I am swept back
> where dead lichens drip . . .
> so for your arrogance
> I am broken at last . . .

Orpheus' mistake in looking back, usually interpreted as eagerness, has here become arrogance; and Eurydice does not even show much wish to return to earth with him:

> if you had let me wait
> I had grown from listlessness into peace,
> if you had let me rest with the dead,
> I had forgot you
> and the past.

This is certainly not the way the story has traditionally been understood; it could even be said that if Orpheus' mistake was caused by male arrogance it is difficult to understand why he went to Hades to rescue her in the first place. A story about the overeagerness of love has been turned into a story of male arrogance (or, if we prefer to read it as a dramatic monologue, not identifying poet and speaker – a reading that seems unlikely for H.D., who usually speaks in her own person – into a story of female resentment). Either way, one of the great tragic love-stories is now about sexual hostility. The poem begins 'So you have swept me back', and the most revealing word is probably the first. Four of the sections begin with 'so': this usage, common enough in colloquial English, means something like 'what I have long suspected has turned out to be true' ('so you're not going to marry him after all'), and it can of course be taken as evidence either of Orpheus' true motives or of Eurydice's long smouldering resentment.

Denise Levertov admired and was influenced by the poems of H.D., but her treatment of the Orpheus story is very different. She treats him, as had often been done before, as a figure for the magical power of poetry:

> Orpheus with his lute made trees
> And the mountain tops that freeze
> Bow themselves when he did sing . . .
> In sweet music is such art,
> Killing care and grief of heart,
> Fall asleep, or hearing die.

This well-known song by John Fletcher (or, perhaps, by Shakespeare) states the traditional view – briefly; but what was it really like to be the enraptured tree? That requires a longer and more exploratory poem.

> *A Tree Telling of Orpheus*
> . . . He was a man, it seemed: the two
> moving stems, the short trunk, the two
> arm-branches, flexible, each with five leafless
>   twigs at their ends . . .

A tree that can bow itself is the subject of legend; of interest to a poet is the tree that can describe the experience – or, indeed, can describe anything. It is not the magical powers of Orpheus that this tree is here describing, it is simply his appearance. Magic is what the legend tells of, but what is needed by the poet is not magic but articulateness. So here is Orpheus' lyre:

> some cut branch bent while it was green,
> strands of a vine tight-stretched across it.   From this,
> when he touched it, and from his voice
> which unlike the wind's voice had no need of our
> leaves and branches to complete its sound,
>   came the ripple.

No magic here, but a powerful imagining of how a tree would understand a musical instrument, something able to produce sounds without needing the wind.

Levertov admired the work of H.D., but they are very different poets. H.D. began as an imagist, writing poems based on the simple idea that a poem should consist of a series of concrete images, avoiding abstractions

> Bitter, bitter jewel
> In the heart of the bowl,

> What is your colour?
> What do you offer
> To us who rebel?

'What do you offer?' the poem asks of the jewel: this might well be
the question which the reader asks of the poem. If we ask it as readers,
we hope for an answer; within the poem, we can be sure no answer will
be allowed to limit the suggestiveness of the image. Because images open
out into so many directions, a succession of images soon becomes inco-
herent if no structure of interpretation is offered. That is why an imagist
poem needs to be short. When H.D. began to write long poems she often
did not change her imagist technique, and the reader who perseveres will
soon get lost. We might be able to supply a structure if the images are
taken from a myth the reader knows, but in H.D.'s long poems we move
from one structure to another: images from *Revelations* alternate with
images from classical mythology, folklore, the Old Testament and (one
sometimes feels) whatever myth suggests itself. I confess that I find her
long poems unreadable.

She also wrote several poems in tribute to friends and mentors, and
her critics tell us who they are addressed to: *The Master*, for instance, is
addressed to Freud, by whom she was analysed.

> I was angry at the old man,
> I wanted an answer,
> a neat answer,
> when I argued and said, 'well, tell me,
> you will soon be dead,
> the secret lies with you,'
> he said,
> 'you are a poet';
>
> I do not wish to be treated like a child, a weakling,
> so I said,
> (I was angry)
> 'you can not last forever . . . '

To the reader who knows something about Freud, and is interested in
the way he treated his patients (and the way they treated him!) this is
fascinating, and throws light on both of them; but it is not possible to
know, unless we are told this by a commentator, that the poem is about
Freud, or that H.D. had been his patient. Since so much of her poetry is

autobiographical – though often in disguised form – the commentators on H D have tended to tell us a good deal about her life, and to offer biographical commentary on her poems.

Denise Levertov is a very different poet, and in my view, a more interesting one. She admired and learned from the work of William Carlos Williams, and was associated with the Black Mountain group of poets, who wrote in free verse, trying to capture the rhythms of American speech in their work. They were mostly men, and to look at their practice through the one prominent female poet among them might give a fresh perspective on a movement that was widespread in America but made little impact on the English poetic scene. The fact that Levertov was born and grew up in England, yet became perhaps the most American of modern female poets, adds an ironic dimension to the situation.

An early poem by her will show her use of speech rhythms:

> *Eros at Temple Stream*
> The river in its abundance
> many-voiced
> all about us as we stood
> on a warm rock to wash
>
> slowly
> smoothing in long
>   sliding strokes
> our soapy hands along each other's
> slippery cool bodies
>
> quiet and slow in the midst of
> the quick of the
> sounding river
>
> our hands were
> flames
> stealing upon quickened flesh until
>
> no part of us but was
> sleek and
> on fire.

All poems are better for reading aloud, but a poem like this needs even more than usual to be spoken aloud, in a way that responds to its sinuous, sensual rhythms. Levertov's own terminology can be useful here. She distinguished three kinds of poetry: that which made use of existing metrical forms, that which sought 'for thought and feeling and perception not experienced as form, a mode of expression that shall maintain that formlessness', and that which 'in thought and feeling and in perception seeks the forms peculiar to those experiences.' She calls the second 'free verse' and the third 'organic form'. That is, of course, a classification that could not have been suggested before the twentieth century, since almost all poems written in earlier centuries would fall into the first group. Free verse has now become so widespread that many young poets simply assume that any use of traditional metrical forms is outmoded, and not for them. Levertov's distinction between 'free verse' and 'organic poetry' is an attempt to reject the formlessness of the former in favour of a poetry whose free movement derives from a faithfulness to the nature of the experience being expressed. *Eros at Temple Stream* she would certainly have considered an example of organic poetry, not of free verse. Any sensitive reader of modern poetry must respect that distinction, but it is not really the same as the distinction between her first category and the other two. Whether a poem is a sonnet or in heroic couplets is not a question of artistic judgement, since a badly written sonnet is still a sonnet; whereas, as she herself admitted, 'most free verse is failed organic poetry'. (In fairness one should add that she later admitted that there is a kind of modern poetry which is written without any desire to seek a form, 'perhaps with the longing to avoid form', though she was clearly sceptical about its value.)

If we ask what gives form to *Eros at Temple* Stream, the answer clearly is its rhythm: it tries to move as the lovers move, with a loving imitation of their gestures and their desire; how far it succeeds must, of course, be the decision of the reader. .It is perhaps worth lingering on the possible response of the old-fashioned lover of traditional form, who might ask how such a poem differs from prose. It is a fair question, which can be answered by asking a further question: would one write an account of such a moment as anything but a poem? It is not, after all, likely to be from a private letter: it is too intimate to be written to a third party, but it could hardly be to the other person involved, who knows about it already; and it does not begin 'Do you remember?', as a letter might. The attempt to describe and record a deeply personal moment is in one sense the very definition of what a poem is.

This poem is typical of Levertov's early work, but in the late sixties she shifted her subject matter. Along with many of her fellow poets she joined in protests against the Vietnam war. It may be illuminating to look at the very widespread movement of protest among poets (not only among poets, of course) through the example of a single person The Vietnam war is now over, and communism is no longer the main bogey of American foreign policy; this should enable us, looking back, to ask how far those protests are dated, and how far the protesters were raising issues of permanent concern.

One of her protest poems includes a quotation from an American major who said 'It became necessary to destroy the town in order to save it', and explained that he was describing the decision to bomb a town, regardless of civilian casualties, in order to rout the Vietcong; the poem then continues:

Language,   coral island
accrued from human comprehensions,
human dreams,

you are eroded as war erodes us.

War is not the only thing that debases language, but it perhaps does so in a particularly complete way; and of course a poet is equipped, perhaps better than anyone else, to point this out. Looking through Levertov's protest poems of the late sixties and the seventies, I am struck by the fact that their most powerful moments are about the brutal absurdities, the oversimplifications of war. Of course they were about a particular war; but just as a love poem may be written to a particular person yet speak to readers who apply it to their own lives, so a protest poem will have a continued life when the war is over because it could be applied to any war.

At this point I must be personal. At the time, I shared the condemnation of American policy in Vietnam, but did not share the tendency of some protesters to go into generalisations about capitalism, and their consequent idealising of communism. Indeed, protest can also erode the language like war: when Levertov writes that there has come a time 'when only anger is love' she too is beginning to use language like that American major.

There is no doubt that the Vietnam protests were enormously important to Levertov. Since that issue is now over, we can ask what remains of permanent value in her anti-war poems. Of course issues like that are in one sense never over, and poems of protest do not necessarily die when the particular issue dies. Many of Levertov's protest poems now seem to ask for a response that discusses the politics of American foreign policy rather than the immediacy of a response to poetry: at the time it could have been hard to separate these, but it is much easier now. So I would like to end on one which still reads like a poem. Feeling that she is returning from her protests to the world, she personifies the world, memorably, as a dog, 'too tired to wag its tail'; the dog 'patiently scratches himself on the front steps', and she is able to let in the world again:

> Where have I been
> without the world? Why am I glad
> he wolfs his food and gathers
> strength for the next journey?

Of course it was not the world that was too tired, it was Levertov's ability to write about the world without having to drop into the mode of protest. It is inevitable that poets should sometimes write about their ability, or their inability, to write poems – or, as here, about the transition from one to the other.

Ways of Being Modern: Edna St Vincent Millay

The distinction between form and content is perhaps the most basic dichotomy in literary criticism. All students of language know – and are often told – that it has only limited usefulness, because what you say is always influenced by the way you say it; but the distinction, though limited, is certainly useful, and I shall now use it to say that the modernism of Moore, H.D. and Levertov is, in their various ways, a matter of form (how a poem uses language), and Millay's is mainly a matter of content.

Edna St Vincent Millay was easily the most popular and the most widely read female poet of her day: her books sold well, her public readings drew huge and enthusiastic audiences; to an interviewer she said 'I think people like my poetry because it is mostly about things that anybody has experienced,' listing love, death, nature and the sea. She also dealt with public themes, and her political poems express a position that most readers of poetry would find sympathetic: pacifist to begin with, shifting, as the horrors of Nazism became clearer, to support of America's entering the war against Hitler. And most strikingly, her poems are sexually outspoken, at a time when that was still daring. 'Outspoken' is not the same as explicit: she does not describe sexual intercourse or use the four-letter words, but she is very frank:

I shall forget you presently, my dear,
So make the most of this, your little day,
Your little month, your little half a year,
Ere I forget, or die, or move away,
And we are done forever; by and by
I shall forget you, as I said, but now
If you entreat me with your loveliest lie
I will protest you with my favourite vow.
I would indeed that love were longer lived,
And vows were not so brittle as they are,
But so it is, and nature had contrived
To struggle on without a break thus far, —
Whether or not we find what we are seeking
Is idle, biologically speaking.

There has long been a tradition of libertine poetry in English, cele-
brating the pleasures of sex without love, of pleasure without
commitment; but the speaker — and indeed the author — of such poems
has always been male. Although there is no internal indication that the
speaker of this poem is a woman, I doubt if anyone ever reads it without
knowing this. The switch in the sex of the speaker makes this a highly
unconventional, indeed a daring poem (for its time, that is: since then we
have had the sexual revolution that Millay was a forerunner of). When
Suckling wrote

Out upon it, I have loved
Three whole days together,
And am like to love three more
If it prove fair weather,

he was striking a posture, writing about himself: the woman he is
enjoying the affair with has no identity. But the recipient of Millay's
poem is a real presence in it, because of the condescension with which
she treats him ('your little day', 'your little half a year') and the certainty
with which she is in control, and enjoying her power. And as well as this
— no doubt connected with it — is the Darwinian touch in the last four
lines, the observation that nature has 'so far' managed to 'struggle on'
without the 'lovely lies': this prepares us for the very unpoetic last line,
where the tossing in of the last two words, taken from a very different
register, is a way of saying that she knows perfectly well that this is not
what one is supposed to say in poetry.

This poem could never have been written before the 20th century. If modernism is a new way of using language in poetry, then there is nothing modernist about this poem; so perhaps we need to say that it is modern but not modernist. This calls attention to the fact that its novelty belongs to the content, not to the language.

Yet although this distinction, between form and content, is useful, even necessary, in discussing poetry, this example shows its limitations. Linguistic choices are always being made, and the attitude to the man, though that is best thought of as content, has led to a switch of register which is just as well classified as form, since register is a linguistic matter.

Millay fell out of favour shortly after her death, and no doubt there are two reasons for this. One is her reputation itself. Alicia Ostriker observed acidly that it happens over and over to women artists that 'to write as a sexual woman is to be immediately popular and then damned by the critics. And as soon as you die, if not a little before.' The other reason is that she was not a modernist: once it was established in literary criticism that the real newness was to use language in a new way, Millay was no longer a figure in the history of modernism. So she was damned for content and damned for form.

Here is another of Millay's coolly contemptuous sonnets:

> I being born a woman and distressed
> By all the needs and notions of my kind,
> Am urged by your propinquity to find
> Your person fair, and feel a certain zest
> To bear your body's weight upon my breast
> So subtly is the fume of life designed,
> To clarify the pulse and cloud the mind,
> And leave me once again undone, possessed.
> Think not for this, however, the poor treason
> Of my stout blood against my staggering brain,
> I shall remember you with love, or season
> My scorn with pity, – let me make it plain:
> I find this frenzy insufficient reason
> For conversation when we meet again.

Though it does not use the word, this poem is even more biological than the other in its outlook: sexual frenzy is attributed to the woman, not to the man, because it is the woman who reproduces (though Millay in fact never had children). The sexual drive is coolly and decisively detached from human companionship, and the man, reduced to an agent of reproduction, need not expect any respect as a person. 'Hope not for mind in woman', wrote Donne in one of his most misogynistic moments; Millay, who knew her Donne, hopes not for mind in men – and does even seem to want it.

The Radicalisation of Gwendolyn Brooks?

Gwendolyn Brooks was the most celebrated black poet of her time; and there is one episode in her life that discussions of her work are almost certain to mention: the fact that in 1967, then aged 50 and already famous, she attended a conference of black writers at Fisk University in Nashville. There she heard younger people declare that 'black poets should write as blacks, about blacks, and address themselves to blacks.' Deeply impressed by their militancy, she regarded the experience as life-changing, and determined in future to put her race at the centre of her experience, and write for blacks.

How far a woman poet should place being a woman at the centre not only of her life but of her writing is a question that has troubled many of the poets discussed in this book. Now we encounter a woman aware of two ways of being disadvantaged, and realising that to be both is not only to be doubly disadvantaged, but to be offered a dilemma: which is more important?

That being a woman was important to Brooks is unquestionable: the poem that shows this most powerfully and most movingly is possibly *The Mother*, which begins

> Abortions will not let you forget.
> You remember the children you got that you did not get . . .

The most powerful effects of word-play in a poem are often the least ingenious: the play upon two different senses in which a woman 'gets' a child, once it has been offered to the reader, seems obvious, and sums up the dilemma of the woman who has had an abortion: her distress seems already to belong in the language, and the poem is simply pointing it out. The rest of the poem develops this idea:

> You were born, you had body, you died.
> It is just that you never giggled or planned or cried.

Just as she got them and did not get them, so they were and were not born. This poem shows – if indeed it needed showing – that writing about being a woman mattered to Brooks; the episode at Fisk matters because it showed her being confronted by the choice between writing as a woman and writing as a black, and deciding that race was more important than gender.

A song in the front yard is a poem of teenage rebellion: the speaker is a young black girl rebelling against her mother's attempt to keep her respectable. The 'front yard' (in the American sense of 'front garden') is where she's been brought up to stay, but 'I want a peek at the back / Where it's rough and untended and hungry weed grows'. Her mother sneers at the untended back yard, but the girl wants a good time:

> And I'd like to be a bad woman, too,
> And wear the brave stockings of night-black lace
> And strut down the streets with paint on my face.

Of De Wit Williams on his way to Lincoln Cemetery is a short and very simple ballad about the male equivalent of this speaker, born in Alabama, bred in Illinois, who was 'nothing but a plain black boy', and (because he was disreputable? because he was black and deprived?) led a life centred on the pool hall, 'Where he picked his women, where He drank his liquid joy', and is now on his way to the cemetery.

The disreputable life that a black girl longs for and a black boy leads has nothing political about it; but such deprivation can easily be politicised, as it is, for instance, in a sonnet beginning 'First fight. Then fiddle':, addressing, this time, not the gaily disreputable but the culturally aspiring:

> Be deaf to music and to beauty blind.
> Win war. Rise bloody, maybe not too late
> For having first to civilize a space
> Wherein to play your violin with grace.

Writing a poem requires choice of subject, and so can address politics directly; but playing the violin cannot; the politically committed violinist cannot combine musical and political action, and must, to some extent, choose between them. And this poem is quite explicit about which comes first: it begins 'first fight; then fiddle.'

These poems – and there are many others like them – seem to be clear illustrations of the change that came over Brooks' work after her experience at that black writers' conference; but they are not. They were all written before 1967, some of them more than 20 years before. She had always written about the experience of American blacks, and she had often shown their alienation from respectable white society. What changed after 1967 was not the sort of poems she wrote, but the life she led: she left her distinguished white publishers, and her books were brought out by the explicitly black Broadside Press of Detroit, she ran workshops for aspiring black writers, she travelled to East Africa, and she succeeded in transforming the 'cold respect' she had experienced at Fisk into enthusiastic acceptance by the young black community. There was really only one important change in her writing, and it concerns not content but form: she now wrote more in free verse, and made less use of the verbal dexterity she had used so skilfully in her earlier verse. This put her more on the wavelength of younger readers – white as well as black.

I shall look at two of the most powerful poems she wrote after 1957, neither, as it happens, very typical, and neither fitting very well into the change brought about by her political conversion. The first is short enough to quote in full:

> We real cool. We
> Left school. We
>
> Lurk late. We
> Strike straight. We
>
> Sing sin. We
> Thin gin. We
>
> Jazz June. We
> Die soon.

The tight-lipped supercilious assurance of the pool players finds a brilliant, wholly unexpected expression in the fact that it is written entirely in monosyllables, rhyming with casual ease and ending each stanza with the single self-assured word that matters most to the pool players (yes, that is what they are, as the sub-title makes clear: '*The Pool Players. Seven at the Golden Shovel*). Or perhaps we should call that the title, since what stands above it is simply the three self-assured words of the first line: 'We real cool'. As for the last line, it is no doubt true (drugs, guns or AIDS makes early death probable enough), and it is hard to decide whether it is an admission or a boast. This poem does more in 24 words than many do in 24 stanzas.

Riot, also post-1967, is very different. The riot it deals with is a race riot, and it begins with an epigraph from Martin Luther King: 'riot is the language of the unheard', which seems to announce a very political poem. But the speaker of this poem is not one of the rioters but one of the victims, John Cabot, a prosperous, cultured, self-satisfied white Southerner. When he sees and hears the rioters swarming towards him, he feels contempt for their grossness along with fear. '"Don't let It touch me! The blackness! Lord!" he whispered / to any handy angel in the sky.' We have already been told that John Cabot was 'once a Wycliffe' (presumably a member of an extreme Protestant sect), and when he calls the black mob 'the blackness' he seems to be running together their race and the fact that they personify evil, and can only be kept off by a divine intervention in which, possibly, he no longer believes. The poem ends

> John Cabot went down in the smoke and fire
> And broken glass and blood, and he cried 'Lord!
> Forgive these nigguhs that know not what they do.

A simple radical poem would show the death of an innocent black man; this poem shows the death of a not-so-innocent rich white. Commentators determined to show how radical Brooks became after 1967 notice only John Cabot's superiority, not the fact that he is killed. It is difficult, perhaps impossible, to decide the attitude of the author behind that ironic, disturbing last line: perhaps Cabot quotes Jesus at the mob because he is forgiving them, perhaps he identifies himself with Christ because he cannot get rid of his conviction of superiority. We are reminded that he is a white southerner by his pronunciation of 'nigguhs': perhaps to show us that he cannot shed his superiority even at the moment of death, perhaps to tell us that he is who is, and cannot help that, and his white superiority cannot help him now. It is very difficult not to insert our own prejudices into the reading of this poem. Or, perhaps, into all Brooks' poems.

Sylvia Plath

Sylvia Plath has shared the same fate as Emily Brontë, that her life story has become more famous than (and has therefore illuminated or – more often – distorted) her poems. But whereas the personal documents about Emily Brontë have to be disinterred by scholars, Plath died in a blare of publicity: we know not too little but too much about her life, her children, her husband, her suicide. This has given rise to some of the most interesting discussions of our time on how her poetry relates to her biography, all of which I propose to ignore. This book has consistently set out to rescue poems from their biographical context, and it will end as it began.

When Plath died in 1963 she had published only one volume, *The Colossus,* which was received with respect but none of the hysteria which her fate and her later poems aroused. Three more volumes followed, and eventually her *Collected Poems,* in 1981, edited with care and tact by her husband, Ted Hughes. That book is all we need. Of course it is uneven, as are almost all books of poems, but it is clear that she was from the beginning a brilliant poet. Choosing a poem to start with is, inevitably, arbitrary, so here is *Mirror.*

> I am silver and exact. I have no preconceptions.
> Whatever I see I swallow immediately
> Just as it is, unmisted by love or dislike.
> I am not cruel, only truthful –
> The eye of a little god, four-cornered.
> Most of the time I meditate on the opposite wall.
> It is pink, with speckles. I have looked at it so long
> I think it a part of my heart. But it flickers.
> Faces and darkness separate us over and over.
> Now I am a lake. A woman bends over me,
> Searching my reaches for what she really is.
> Then she turns to those liars, the candles or the moon.
> I see her back, and reflect it faithfully.
> She rewards me with tears and an agitation of hands.
> I am important to her. She comes and goes.
> Each morning it is her face that replaces the darkness.
> In me she has drowned a young girl, and in me an old woman
> Rises toward her day after day, like a terrible fish.

'I have no preconceptions': the mirror is rather pleased with itself, proud of the fidelity with which it shows back what is shown to it. The wit of the poem is based on the conceit that the mirror knows what it is doing, and has a range of human emotions – pride, resentment, even fear at what it reflects. The disturbing material is only present indirectly: the mirror reflects it without, perhaps, realising its power. In the light of the later, darker poems, this one takes on a deeper resonance. Are we to believe that the woman who bends over the mirror is the author? If so, she is not yet 30 when she looks in the mirror and sees her own reflection as an old woman rising towards her 'like a terrible fish'. The intensity that was recorded direct in some of the fierce terrible poems of *Ariel* is implied in this controlled and witty poem.

The common view of Plath's development – that her earlier, more controlled poems gave way to the far more powerful and personal work of the last year or two of her life – is at best a half-truth. There is a good deal of intensity in her earlier work, and a good deal of control in the best of her later work. (The fact that we can speak of 'early' and 'later' work in a career that lasted about seven years is a sign of how rapidly she developed.) *Lorelei* is an 'earlier' poem which retells its legend with great power. The Lorelei is the fatally beautiful woman of German legend who by her singing from her mountain fastness over the river Rhine lures sailors to their death in a whirlpool: and she has lured women poets to echo her spell-binding song – both Plath and, as we shall see, Stevie Smith. The fatal lure of a siren's song is a subject that seems to be waiting for Plath, obsessed as she was with the horrible beauty of dying. This poem blends the death wish with a cool awareness of its folly:

> Sisters, your song
> Bears a burden too weighty
> For the whorled ear's listening
> Here, in a well-steered country,
> Under a balanced ruler . . .

The impudent assurance of the pun 'well-steered' (applying both to the country and the fisherman's boat) reminds us of detachment while mocking it slightly; like all her best poetry it neither surrenders to hysteria nor escapes from it. The poem, like the legend, does of course end on a death wish, as the fisherman drowns: its haunting last line is 'Stone, stone, ferry me down there.'

Plath's two best-known poems are probably 'Daddy' and 'Lady Lazarus'. Both have autobiographical content, brilliantly used, but, alas, an easy invitation to readers to treat them as biographical documents rather than as poems, though the fact that much of the apparently autobiographical material is clearly untrue acts as a natural brake on this. In both poems the short lines, the repetitions, the exclamatory sentences are an invitation to a rapid, intense, breathless reading. They have much in common with the 'confessional poetry' that was very popular in the later twentieth century, though their very intensity sweeps us along in a way that invites us to wonder how reliable they are.

Plath's father, Otto Plath, who was German and came to America in at the age of 16, died when Sylvia was 8; the 'Daddy' who figures in her poem is almost entirely a fiction of her imagination, as the poem more or less admits ('Daddy, I have had to kill you. / You died before I had time'). She imagines him as a Nazi, and imagines herself as a Jew – both fictions, as the reader can guess from the hysterically vivid lines of the poem:

> I have always been scared of *you*,
> With your Luftwaffe, your gobbledygook,
> And your neat moustache
> And your Aryan eye, bright blue.
> Panzer-man, panzer-man, O You.

The fact that Plath tried to commit suicide when she was 20 (as is wittily and frighteningly described in her brilliant novel *The Bell Jar*) can hardly have had anything to do with the long dead Otto, but the hysterical poem is not pulled up by mere questions of fact:

> But they pulled me out of the sack,
> And they stuck me together with glue.
> And then I knew what to do.
> I made a model of you,
> A man in black with a Meinkampf look . . .

'I made a model of you': this could describe something she actually did at the time, or it could be telling him (us) that the father figure who inhabits her imagination and appears in her poems was her own 'model' of Otto Plath. Much of the power of 'Daddy' derives from our uncertainty whether she is really talking about Otto or obviously making up a fictitious version of him. The poem, indeed, is full of uncertainties, though its insistent rhythm and air of assertion seem to be signs of great certainty. The last line catches the mood of the whole poem: 'Daddy, daddy, you bastard, I'm through.' 'Through' is of course colloquial American for 'finished', and could mean either that the poem is finished or that the poet is finished – worn out, or suicidal. At the same time it suggests 'through with you' – not wanting anything more to do with you. These are not the careful ambiguities of a witty poem, but the breathless ambiguity of someone screaming: evidence both that the poem is breathlessly colloquial and also that it is very carefully poised.

'Lady Lazarus' (written only two or three weeks later) is a kind of companion piece to 'Daddy' – even more powerful, more hysterical and yet more controlled: a controlled poem, that is, filled with uncontrolled hysteria. Written only weeks before her actual suicide, this poem presents her own dying as a public and theatrical performance:

> The big strip tease.
> Gentlemen, ladies
>
> These are my hands
> My knees.
> I may be skin and bone,
> Nevertheless, I am the same, identical woman

This brassy tone is addressed to 'the peanut-crunching crowd', which 'shoves in to see' the circus performance that is at the same time all too real. There can be few readers of this poem who do not know that its author did actually commit suicide a short time later. I shall conclude by asking the impossible but necessary question, Does this enrich or damage their response? Is it possible, is it desirable, is it (perhaps) necessary, to separate literature from its biographical origins?

On Sunday 10 February 1963 Sylvia Plath put her two children to bed upstairs, sealed their bedroom to prevent gas getting in, and gassed herself in the kitchen. The poems she wrote in the last week or so of her life have dates attached to them in the *Collected Poems*. The very last (dated 5 February) is called 'Edge':

> The woman is perfected.
> Her dead
>
> Body wears the smile of accomplishment,
> The illusion of a Greek necessity
>
> Flows in the scrolls of her toga,
> Her bare
>
> Feet seem to be saying:
> We have come so far, it is over.
>
> Each dead child coiled, a white serpent,
> One at each little
>
> Pitcher of milk, now empty.
> She has folded

Them back into her body as petals
Of a rose close when the garden

Stiffens and odours bleed
From the sweet, deep throats of the night flower.

The moon has nothing to be sad about,
Staring from her hood of bone.

She is used to this sort of thing.
Her blacks crackle and drag.

The Phoenix was a legendary bird that built its own funeral pyre, then lit it and committed suicide, only to rise again from the ashes and live another hundred years until it was time to repeat the same process. It has seemed to poets a symbol of Christian resurrection, of the immortality of poetry, or of the lure of suicide; and Sylvia Plath has become the phoenix of women's poetry: 'she is used to this sort of thing.' This is a is a very literary poem: the dead woman is imagined wearing a toga, as if she was a figure from Greek tragedy; the two children coiled at her empty breasts are compared to the snakes that Shakespeare's Cleopatra used for her suicide. And it is also a very personal poem – as intensely personal as a poem can get, written less than a week before her actual suicide.

Did the poet herself separate the poem from its origins? In a sense, the question is unanswerable – or rather, the answer has to be No and Yes. If the author had not been feeling suicidal, the poem would not have been written, so separation is impossible; but if the poem is written, not simply for the poet herself and perhaps those who know her well, but for you and me, it cannot assume that we know what is happening. It is always possible to read a poem in ignorance of its biographical origin, even ignorant of who wrote it: or rather it is always possible in principle, but in an age when biographies of modern poets – and of Victorian novelists – are as widely read as the novels and poems they wrote (perhaps more widely read) not many readers will be able to attain this valuable ignorance. Plath's fame, and the fame of her suicide, derive from her poems, but the fame threatens to swallow (even, one sometimes feels to destroy) the poems.

Only a few days earlier she wrote a poem called 'Kindness':

Kindness glides about my house.
Dame Kindness, she is so nice!

163

This is another very personal poem – Sylvia's friends were very kind to her in the last week of her life – and also another very literary poem: 'Dame Kindness' is not only a mention of the kindness of her friends, it is also imported into the poem from the tradition of Dame Kind, another term for Mother Nature, a figure from Chaucer, from medieval tradition generally, or (more immediately) from Auden. The last stanza of this poem begins 'And here you come, with a cup of tea': who is 'you'? Is it one of the friends who were so kind to her in her last days? Is it her husband, who had deserted her, but who had indeed 'hand[ed] her two children, two roses', as the last line of the poem tells us? Or is it the reader, whose sympathy is aroused by the poem, who in the end is the one who feels only kindness towards her? You and I, freed from the painful personal situation, knowing about it only from the poem, or pretending to know it only from the poem, granting to the poem its true status, freed from the particularities of biography?

The English

Elizabeth Daryush

Elizabeth Daryush was the daughter of Robert Bridges, poet laureate for the first third of the 20th century, whose poetry is rather conventional and conservative. It is not easy to decide if these adjectives apply to her work too. Her 'experiments' with syllabic metre, in which the line is determined by the number of syllables, not of stresses, do not produce effects that seem very different from traditional verse patterns, and in an age of free verse and modernist techniques she now looks like a very traditional poet.

Are the social attitudes of her poems also traditional and conservative? Critics seem divided about this, and it is easy to see why. Here is her best known poem, *Still-Life*:

> Through the open French window the warm sun
> lights up the polished breakfast-table, laid
> round a bowl of crimson roses, for one –
> a service of Worcester porcelain, arrayed
> near it a melon, peaches, figs, small hot
> rolls in a napkin, fairy rack of toast,
> butter in ice, high silver coffee pot,
> and, heaped on a salver, the morning's post.

She comes over the lawn, the young heiress,
From her early walk in her garden wood
Feeling that life's a table set to bless
Her delicate desires with all that's good,

That even the unopened future lies
Like a love-letter, full of sweet surprise.

This is a conventional Shakespearean sonnet, with an orthodox rhyme-scheme, written in syllabics: that is, there are ten syllables in every line, but not arranged in an orthodox iambic pattern. More important than this metrical question is the careful depiction of a rich and elegant life-style: every detail of the breakfast is immaculately correct, we are told with accurate, even fastidious, care what kind of porcelain, what colour roses (not just red, but, more discriminatingly, crimson); we are reminded that the young heiress took her morning walk not just in 'the wood' but in 'her wood'. It is a picture of privilege.

Of course it is always possible for the reader to see this as a picture of a doomed class, and to describe it as suffocating and artificial – as some readers have. But is the poem telling us that? Does it contain an aware-ness of the doom? It tells us that the unopened future is full of 'sweet surprise'? That hardly sounds like doom; but then that might refer to what the heiress expects to find, whereas the actual future will contain dispos-session, even revolution. This poem, with its deeply conservative acceptance of the status quo, can of course be read as a quiet threat of revolution, but the threat will come from the reader. The elegance of a privileged lifestyle can always be seen, by the radical, as doomed: and the more perfectly it is caught by the poet, the more thoroughly the young heiress's awareness dominates the poem, the better the ammunition offered to the reader who is a radical. Does the poem control the reader, or does the reader control the poem?

And does it change our view to find that Daryush also wrote a sonnet called *Children of Wealth,* which tells them that they 'cannot tell / What winter means' because they are protected by privilege, urges them to 'Go down, go out to elemental wrong', and concludes by threatening them with 'horror's wrecking fire', because their home 'is wired within for this, in every room.' It looks as if the radical reader whom I imagined, the revolutionary who reads *Still Life* as a picture of doomed privilege, could be Daryush herself.

Every poem deserves to be read with care, with loving attention; but no poem can be completely protected from politics.

Ruth Pitter

Ruth Pitter, like Edna St Vincent Millay, was a modern woman who wrote about the modern world but showed little influence from the modernist movement. In one way she was even more traditional than Millay, since she wrote lovingly and knowledgably about nature: as a result she is sometimes classed with the Georgians, and regarded as an old-fashioned sentimentalist. This is not altogether unfair to her, but is extremely unfair to the Georgians, many of whom were acutely aware of the modern world, though not very interested in modernist poetry.

> The blear smoke crawls, the dawn glimmers, the children
> With their wan mothers, creep from dens that hide them
> A little from their terror; they turn homeward
> To the poor dole of food allotted strictly,
> To each his portion, just and insufficient;
> To the grey day; labouring on till evening,
> Then turning blindly to the earth for harbour
> As beasts do, bolting into holes in terror.

Nobody could accuse these lines of Pitter's about Londoners during the Second World War of not being aware of the modern world: their account of the fear and deprivation of those who endured air-raids, war-work and rationing is fiercely realistic, even angry: the last two lines reduce the crowd going into an air-raid shelter to beasts 'bolting into holes in terror'. The blear smoke might crawl in a poem by T. S. Eliot, but that would be because of the poet's modernist vision; in Ruth Pitter's poem it is because there is a war on. She could even be accused of being so angry that she exaggerates: 'To each his portion, just and insufficient' is a brilliant account of rationing, but nutritionists are more likely to tell us that the British diet was healthier during rationing than it now is.

It is hardly surprising to learn that this stanza comes from a poem about London in the Second World War; but it might be surprising to learn that the poem is called 'The Cygnet: a Song of Thames', and that a swan is the main character. The life cycle of the swan is interwoven with the pollution caused by industrialisation and war, and the result is one of Pitter's most ambitious poems. It opens:

> He sails alone, rocking on turbid water,
> Water that has been fouled by wicked creatures . . .

There the wicked creatures appear to be the Londoners themselves, 'fouling' by their industrialising. It is not surprising that a poem about the blitz should say 'The fiery rain is falling', but lines like the following can give us pause:

> White sheets of light flicker and flap and vanish
> The steel-blue fingers, stark, intent and rigid,
> Deliberately seek their prey in heaven.

This description of searchlight beams does not distinguish them as being more virtuous than the wicked German bombing, but assimilates it to the unnatural activity taking place everywhere around the innocence of the cygnet.

Poems about nature – whether by the Georgians or from earlier times – are often enriched by being not only about the natural scene, but also about the watcher, and the act of watching. One of Pitter's most praised nature poems, *Stormcock in Elder*, describes a bird that made its nest in an elder tree growing over the roof of her broken down cottage, 'Scarcely an arm's length from the eye', so that the careful, accurate description of the bird includes an awareness of the watcher:

> The throbbing throat that made the cry,
> The breast dewed from the misty air,
> The polished bill that opened wide
> And showed the pointed tongue inside.

She watches, and we watch with her.

Though Pitter was never a popular poet, she did reach out to a wide audience when she accepted the commission of regularly sending a poem to *Woman,* a popular magazine with a readership of nine million. The editor has described the meeting, uneasy at first, at which she and Pitter explored the possibility of this commission, and how the reservations they had both begun with melted away as the relationship grew more harmonious and the commission more possible, Almost any poet – along with most editors – is likely to view such a commission ambivalently, delight at poetry reaching such a wide audience clashing with unease at the thought that it could result in sentimentalised or over-simplifying poems. Nobody would be able to pick out from Pitter's Collected Poems just which ones had appeared in the magazine, but no-one is likely to be surprised that one of them was *The Sparrow's Skull.*

The skull is in my hand, the minute cup of bone,
And I remember her, the tame, the loving one,
Who came in at the window, and seemed to have a mind
More towards sorrowful man than to those of her own kind.

Did it need Pitter's talent to write this? The first line is promising, with some of her cool observation, but the second, with its trite adjectives, could have been written by any of a score of 'nature poets', and the second couplet offers a very easy example of the pathetic fallacy. This poem carries a sub-title 'Memento Mori. Written at the Fall of France', which thrusts upon us not only the occasion of the poem's writing, but an underlining of the connection between the nature poem and the human situation, as if the poet is anxious lest we miss it. How does the writer of such a poem steer the necessary course between writing down to its audience on the one hand, and on the other an overanxious snobbery, dreading lest the poem be too easily understood? Of course there are dangers for poetry when poets write for popular magazines, but the gain is much greater.

Here to conclude is the opening couplet of Pitter's sonnet, *The Beautiful Negress*:

Her gait detached her from the moving throng:
Like night, advancing with long pace and slow . . .

Almost as much as the poem itself, I love the comment on it by another poet, James Kirkup, who claimed 'this poem gives to a T my dear old friend Madame Sheba . . . as she used to sweep along Tottenham Court Road, carrying all before, and behind, her . . . ' Such comments are, surely, worth more than a careful analysis of the slow, dignified movement of the second line, though perhaps they are most likely to be made by a reader who feels such movement. Of course the poem is dated: it is no longer unusual to see a black woman walking up Tottenham Court Road, and it is no longer quite acceptable to call her a Negress; but good poems can shrug off such datemanship.

Kathleen Raine

Kathleen Raine was long-lived, prolific, learned and even formidable. She published a dozen volumes of poetry, several volumes of autobiography, and at least fourteen books of criticism, including four studies of

William Blake. Admirers of her poetry have no doubt that she is the most important woman poet of the 20th century (an opinion she shared).

Raine's prose is both polemical and reactionary, often denouncing 'the meaningless tasks created by a soulless technocracy', and will seem wise to those who share its views and commonplace to those who don't. Although she studied biology at university, one of her best-known poems, *Amo Ergo Sum*, can be read as a kind of anti-scientific statement, offering the awareness of nature of someone who loves rather than studies it.

> Because I love
> The earth upon her astral spindle winds
> Her ecstasy-producing dance.

> Because I love
> Clouds travel on the winds through wide skies,
> Skies wide and beautiful and deep.

Keats complained two hundred years earlier that 'all charms fly At the mere touch of cold philosophy' (by 'philosophy' he meant more or less what we mean by 'science'); he claimed that philosophy will 'unweave a rainbow', relegating it to 'the dull catalogue of common things'. Whether or not Raine was remembering these lines, she is carrying on what they said, and has found a better way to say it: Keats' lines seem merely a grumble compared with her splendidly positive assertion: she offers a creative parody of Descartes' famous proposition 'Cogito ergo sum: I think, therefore I am.' It's a splendid idea for a poem; but the writing does not, alas, live up to the idea: the adjectives describing the 'wide skies' all sound rather ordinary, and as we read on it gets no better:

> Because I love
> Wind blows white sails,
> The wind blows over flowers, the sweet wind blows.

That Nature offers her beauties 'because she loves' is a powerful idea, but the verbal dress of the beauties is very ordinary: the wind is simply –and unmemorably – 'the sweet wind'.

Farewell Happy Fields, the first volume of her autobiography, has the charm that memories of childhood often have: 'Never, in later life, do we experience that sense of perfect arrival that is, in childhood, the term of every walk; we bring the whole of ourselves to the very place; . . . our thought is what we see and love and touch.'. True; and readers are often grateful to the sensitive writer who produces the story of her childhood, offering us the sort of memories we all cherish. Here is the material for poetry – material it is not always easy to make into poems.

In *Heirloom* Raine explores this task by attributing it to her mother. 'She gave me childhood's flowers', the poem begins, then continues by listing the memories that the mother passed on to her. Then the third stanza tells us:

> Gave me her memories,
> But kept her last treasure:
> 'When I was a lass,' she said,
> Sitting among the heather,
> Suddenly I saw
> That all the moor was alive!
> I have told no-one before.'

Once again, the poem fails to live up to its conception: this no doubt almost mystical experience which the mother now passes on, assuring the child how important it was, is given in very prosaic language. We are told that she 'knew all', and spent the rest of her days 'treasuring the price-less pearl' – alas, the most commonplace of metaphors. I have no doubt that the moment was important for both mother and daughter: but we have only their assurance that it was so. For poetry to emerge, significant experiences need to find significant language.

Raine's best poems often seem to me the tiny ones, those in which a happy thought or image came to her, and did not have to be sustained at any length: I choose Euridice as an example, since we have already looked at two poems about this mythical figure and her husband Orpheus: two ambitious poems, compared to which this tiny gem seems unimportant – but brilliant.

> What substance had Euridice,
> Or shade?
> Unseen he knew that she was near
> Whom when with bodily arms he held
> Was waterfall, was fleeting flame, was empty air:
> Yet in that country far
> He only cast a shadow, bright was she.

Euridice seems to have changed for a moment into Proteus, the shape-changer, and Orpheus' grief when she vanished has changed into a different kind of bafflement. So learned a woman as Raine is not likely to have muddled her legends, so the poem must be deliberately surprising, as if to convey the bewilderment of Orpheus. Another short poem offering only a single thought is *Turner's Seas*, which explores the paradox that Turner's paintings of storm and shipwreck, often terrifying, are seen by us as beautiful. Like Turner, Raine does not flinch from the horror:

> Men and women like spindrift hurled in spray
> And no survivors in those sliding glassy graves.

And, to conclude, the shortest poem of all, offering just one thought:

> On its way I see
> The anew created
> Garden as old as woman; to me
> These daisies in the grass are shown, these
> Birds in the apple tree:
> Is my sin, then,
> Forgiven?

This poem seems to me to hinge on an ambiguity that is not settled, and that we do not wish to settle: is the poet speaking, or are we to assume it is Eve speaking? It could be a tiny dramatic monologue: Eve dreams of returning to the garden and finding it flourishing again. Or the poet sees any garden and remembers Eden, remembers that Nature was tainted by the fall, and moved by its beauty she imagines that innocence is back. One conceit, one short poem, nothing more needed. It is a beautiful uncertainty.

Stevie Smith

It is difficult to imagine a greater contrast than that between Kathleen Raine and the quirky, impudent, witty, naïve (or faux-naïf?) work of Stevie Smith. Smith was more than a comic poet, but she could be very funny; so we can begin with what is certainly a funny poem:

> *The Jungle Husband*
> Dearest Evelyn, I often think of you
> Out with the guns in the jungle stew
> Yesterday I hittapotamus

I put the measurements down for you but they got lost in the fuss
It's not a good thing to drink out here
You know, I've practically given it up dear.
Tomorrow I am going alone a long way
Into the jungle. It is all gray
But green on top
Only sometimes when a tree has fallen
The sun comes down plop, it is quite appalling.
You never want to go into a jungle pool
In the hot sun, it would be the act of a fool
Because it's always full of anacondas, Evelyn, not looking ill-fed
I'll say. So no more now from your loving husband, Wilfred.

Poor Wilfred: he is clearly no David Attenborough, and doesn't understand much about the jungle. The poem is said to have put audiences into fits of laughter, and to comment on it must run the risk of sounding pompous. Is Wilfred really in the jungle? It's in one sense a meaningless question (what does 'really' mean, in a poem like this?), but it's tempting to place this layman's jungle in Wilfred's imagination. Why should he be imagining it? Clearly something is wrong: was he drinking too much? 'You know I've practically given it up dear' could sound anxious, as if he doesn't really expect to be believed, and Stevie herself remarked at a reading that he had had too much to drink. Had Evelyn had enough of him, and told him to go jump in the lake: hence he assures her that it's full of the largest, most bad-tempered of snakes with the longest, most formidable name: 'you wouldn't really want me to do that, Evelyn?' Poor Wilfred, it's hard not to like him – as long as we aren't married to him.

Stevie Smith wrote a good deal, and not all her poems come off: those that are *faux-naif*, long-winded or (more frequently) too short-winded, are the price for her quirky successes. Nor will readers always agree on which are the successes: this is no doubt inevitable with such eccentricities, but there are some clear favourites, and there is something like universal agreement that the best of all is 'Not Waving but Drowning'. This poem about a dead man who feels he was misunderstood depends on two brilliant insights. First, that a swimmer's gesture when drowning could easily be misunderstood: the waving arm could just be a greeting, not a call for help. The perception might have occurred to others, but no-one has put it so tersely. And second (this of course is one of poetry's basic devices) that familiar expressions (he swam too far out) can be taken literally or figuratively: 'I was much too far out all my life', he complains.

Both these insights are obvious – once they've been written down. All brilliant poetic touches are obvious, once they've been written down.

Interpreters of Stevie Smith's poems are always in danger of feeling foolish: not only because anyone translating a poem into prose commentary is likely to sound laboured, but particularly in her case, where the poem both sounds naïve and (often) isn't, whereas the commentary doesn't sound naïve but perhaps is. So it is a kind of comfort to find her in the role of the laboured interpreter of the naïve:

> Our Bog is dood, our Bog is dood,
>   They lisped in accents mild,
> But when I asked them to explain
>   They grew a little wild.
> How do you know your Bog is dood
>   My darling little child?

Being children, they are clearly mispronouncing: probably trying to say 'our God is good', but this obvious explanation is kept out of sight. The children, like the obstinate poet, insist on being subjective ('We know because we wish it so'), and it turns out that they don't agree among themselves what it means. The poet ends by delighting in her inability to understand. The poem has defeated both poet and children, and it concludes with an almost frightening ambiguity: the encroaching sea will drown them but it 'never yet drowned me'. Or so she thinks. 'Our Bog is Dood' looks like a poem about the battle between understanding and the impossibility of understanding, and it's impossible to say which wins. To read it like that fits with the author's well-known mischievousness.

All her favourite poems are short, not only because favourite poems are often short, but because her flashes of insight tend to be sudden and brief. One flash of insight led her to identify herself with a frog (the opposite to a princess, therefore, in folk tales, a princess in disguise), and this she kept up for slightly longer. 'I am a frog,' she tells us; she lives 'at the bottom / Of a green well'. By the third stanza the poem has grown self-conscious:

> The story is familiar
> Everybody knows it well
> But do other enchanted people feel as nervous
> As I do? The stories do not tell.

That, of course, sets her going: Stevie Smith's subject, over and over, is what the stories do not tell. In this case, they do not tell that the frog may not really have wanted to turn into a prince. Or rather, that he did and didn't want it: 'It will be heavenly To be set free', as he realises, but not everyone wants to be heavenly:

> Only disenchanted people
> Can be heavenly.

If you're locked up in a fairy tale you are still enchanted, and to be enchanted is to belong to the world of poetry, whereas to be heavenly is to belong to the world of happy endings.

Such teasing, eccentric poems, so often refusing to state a conclusion, refusing to let on whether they mean what they say, suggest a poet who refuses to declare herself. Yet in fact Stevie Smith was, on occasion, quite willing to declare herself, above all about religion. She had an Anglican upbringing, her sister was a devout Catholic, she was in some moods deeply attracted by the rituals of Christianity, yet when she wrote in sober prose she could be as savage in her attacks on Christianity as William Empson or Richard Dawkins. She described her lecture on 'The Necessity of not Believing' as 'not at all whimsical . . . but serious'. When it was published it naturally drew fierce criticism from churchmen, and she defended it vigorously: she described Christianity as a 'hell-haunted religion', and grew impatient with those who tried to evade or deny the fact that for many centuries Christianity has consigned unbelievers and heretics (sometimes the vast majority of mankind) to eternal torment. So her poems about Christianity are sometimes less teasing, and more straightforward, than she usually is: when she begins a poem 'Oh Christianity, Christianity, / Why do you not answer our difficulties?' she really does want answers, and is serious in her impatience at not getting them. Another poem ends, again with complete seriousness:

> This god the Christians show
> Out with him, out with him, let him go.

She is so free with capital letters, that it can hardly be an accident that 'god' does not rate one here.

Now if we turn back to 'Our Bog is Dood' we can see that it may well be a more serious poem than I suggested. Those children who cannot even pronounce, and certainly can't understand, the theological assertion they have been made to sing, are a kind of parody of the theologians. Theology is full of terms whose meaning is disputed: similarly the children can never agree 'what was dood and what their Bog'. Their childish theology is not really less sophisticated than the confident assertions of theologians, it just exposes the naivety.

Bert Brecht's famous *Fragen eines Lesenden Arbeiters* (Questions of a Working Man who reads) puts, in all seriousness, the questions that conventional history teachers refrain from asking:

> Der junge Alexander eroberte Indien.
> Er allein?
> (Young Alexander conquered India,
> – alone?)

Several of Stevie Smith's poems against Christianity adopt a similar strategy, presenting the other half of a dialogue with orthodoxy: her poem on Jesus asks a series of awkward questions to suggest that being God as well as man must have made his suffering less, not worse, and concludes

> A god is Man's doll, you ass,
> He makes him up like this on purpose

(The use of capitals is certainly not accidental here.)

I doubt if she knew Brecht's poem, but she certainly knew more about foreign literatures (French, Latin, German) than a hasty reader would realise. I take as one example her rendering of Heine's ballad *die Lorelei,* which is both very free and oddly faithful. The Lorelei is the beautiful maiden who sits on a rock overlooking the Rhine and with her singing lures the boatman to his death by drowning; Sylvia Plath turned the story into a very Plath-like poem, and Stevie's version is unmistakeably like one of her poems:

> An antique story comes to me
> And fills me with anxiety,
> I wonder why I fear so much
> What surely has no modern touch?

Heine's poem (translated literally) begins: 'I don't know what it means that I feel so sad. I can't get an old folk tale out of my head.' The sophisticated Heine here sounds more straightforward than the famously naïve Stevie, who not only elaborates her puzzlement at being moved by an old folk tale, but returns to it (as Heine doesn't) at the end:

175

> This story brings me so much grief
> I know not how to find relief.
> Lurks there some meaning underneath?

Which, we may ask, is more sophisticated: to confess one's puzzlement or to say nothing more about it?

It is difficult not to be personal with so quirky a poet, so I will end with *I remember*, simply because it is my favourite among all her poems:

> It was my bridal night I remember,
> An old man of seventy-three
> I lay with my young bride in my arms,
> A girl with t.b.
> It was wartime and overhead
> The Germans were making a particularly heavy raid on Hampstead.
> What rendered the confusion worse, perversely
> Our bombers had chosen that moment to set out for Germany.
> Harry, do they ever collide?
> I do not think it has ever happened,
> Oh my bride, my bride.

Stevie Smith never reached 73, was not a man, and never had a bridal night – all of which may have helped her to invent this comically absurd situation: absurd and yet strangely touching that there is such a mismatch in age and such an absurdly inappropriate setting for a bridal night. The most famous interruption to passion is Mrs Shandy's question 'Did you remember to wind the clock?', leading her husband to complain 'Did ever woman, since the creation of the world, interrupt a man with such a silly question?', but this one deserves to be equally famous (and I would not consider it impossible that Stevie had Mrs Shandy in mind); but the interruption prods the speaker not to annoyance but to passion. It is perhaps the most touching moment in all her poems.

Aurora Leigh *or What is it like to be a woman poet?*

Aurora Leigh is the story of a woman poet, written by a woman poet. Its subject is so close to the concerns of this book that I decided to save it to the end, hoping it would make a fitting conclusion.

Aurora Leigh is a young girl, born in Italy of an English father and an Italian mother, who is orphaned and brought up by her very prim and very English aunt. The division in her between loyalty to Italy, where she was a child, and England, where she grows up, provides the theme of the opening books.

Italy versus England

'Versus' may seem a strong word, but the two countries are certainly presented as competing for the soul of Aurora. Coming to England as a girl, she misses the grandeur of Italy:

> Not a grand nature. Not my chestnut woods
> Of Vallombrosa, cleaving by the spurs
> To the precipices. Not my headlong leaps
> Of waters, that cry out for joy or fear
> In leaping through the palpitating pines,
> Like a white soul tossed out to eternity
> With thrills of time upon it.   (I, 615)

The 'grand nature' of Italy is presented through a paradox: the emphasis is upon impersonality, on the way the sublime landscape ignores the human watcher – even more strongly when she later returns to Italy and sees the Tuscan hills 'As if God verily made you for yourselves And would not interrupt your life with ours'. Yet the images that present this grand nature are imbued with the pathetic fallacy, so that the chestnut woods 'cleave' to the precipice, the waters 'cry out for joy or fear' and are compared to a 'white soul', as if the way to describe nature's indepen-

177

dence of humanity is to present her as a human being taking no notice of us. Even the mention of Vallombrosa is there, surely, to recall one of Milton's most famous similes: it is through what previous poets have told us that we know about Nature's independence from the poets. These lines are firmly in the Romantic tradition: the vast vague longing associated with the headlong leaps of waters would be quite at home in Wordsworth. But they also remind us that there is no complete escape from the human, that nature's independence is perceived *by us*.

The English landscape, as she gets to know it, has a different kind of charm for Aurora: intimate, domestic, and intensely green:

> I had a little chamber in the house,
> As green as any privet hedge a bird
> Might choose to build in, though the nest itself
> Could show but dead-brown sticks and straws; the walls
> Were green, the carpet was pure green, the straight
> Small bed was curtained greenly, and the folds
> Hung green about the window, which let in
> The outdoor world with all its greenery.
> You could not push your head out and escape
> A dash of dawn-dew from the honeysuckle,
> But so you were baptised into the grace
> And privilege of seeing.   (I, 567)

Italy expands, England confines. These fascinating lines combine the feeling of being shut in with the suggestion that art is imitating nature, that the interior of the room is an invitation to look out and respond to the greenery outside. Green is the colour of self-sufficiency, of spontaneous growth, but it can be imitated, and the chamber can take on the intensity of the world outside the window. Both passages explore the relation between the human and the natural worlds, and both are based on the impossibility of conceiving the latter except in terms of the former; but this does not render the contrast any less real. Italian nature rebuffs us, English nature invites us in. The Italian mountains do not ask to be climbed, the English trees greet us as we open a window onto them.

In the end Italy, since the poem ends there, could be said to win. Aurora returns to Italy in Book VII, an experience that is both rediscovery and bewilderment:

> I knew the birds
> And insects – which looked fathered by the flowers

> And emulous of their hues: I recognised
> The moths, with that great overpoise of wings
> Which makes a mystery of them how at all
> They can stop flying.   (VII, 1053)

Even the passing image of 'fathered' may be a glimpse of Aurora's feelings, since Italy is the country where she had known her father; and those unstable, tottering moths can easily be an image for Aurora's own toppling emotion as she rediscovers the intensities of her Italian childhood. As she wanders through the crowded streets of Florence, however, she experiences a 'perfect solitude of foreign lands': knowing nobody, she is alienated but strangely happy. We as readers are being prepared for the final meeting with Romney and the winding up of the plot, though on a first reading we are no more aware of this than Aurora is. And so Book VII ends with a hushed passage that seems to embody the experience of waiting when one does not know one is waiting:

> I did not write, nor read, nor even think,
> But sat absorbed amid the quickening glooms,
> Most like some passive broken lump of salt
> Dropped in by chance to a bowl of oenomel,
> To spoil the drink a little and lose itself
> Dissolving slowly, slowly, until lost.   (VII, 1306)

Aurora's Education

Aurora's experience of England is not only a meeting with the landscape, it is also an education; and the account of her upbringing by the aunt who leads 'a harmless life she called a virtuous life' is satire of a delicacy not often associated with Victorian writing. The first glimpse of the aunt is of her standing outside her country house ('Her somewhat narrow forehead braided tight, As if for taming accidental thoughts'), and then follows a marvellously detailed account of what Aurora was required to learn:

> I danced the polka and Cellarius,
> Spun glass, stuffed birds, and modelled flowers in wax,
> Because she liked accomplishments in girls.   (I, 424)

'Accomplishments', the term that summed up female education in the early 19th century, were what made a girl marriageable – not, of course,

179

that it was proper to admit to so blunt a definition, for a society in which women have no career but marriage protects the self-esteem of its young girls by the pretence that the wish to marry comes from the man, and is received by the female with becoming surprise.

> Aurora's aunt 'liked a woman to be womanly',
> And English women, she thanked God and sighed
> (Some people always sigh in thanking God),
> Were models to the universe.   (I, 444)

Old maids have always offered an easy target for male mockery, and the literary convention that moves towards marriage as the necessary fulfilment for women will be tempted to join in and mock. But the female writer who both believes that the need for love is the most overriding of needs for a woman and also dislikes the cruelty of male mockery ('the marriage market is overstocked,' remarks one of Charlotte Brontë's superior young men) will find herself in a dilemma. Such dilemmas are of course both a problem and an opportunity for the writer, leading to the rich contradiction of Aurora writing of love 'with unkissed lips'.

'I too have my vocation'

By Victorian standards, we are all feminists now. How then do we read this text, in which the heroine struggles against the prevailing assumption that a woman's function can only be that of wife and mother. This view is put forward by Aurora's cousin Romney, who happens to find a notebook of hers, and tells her, with a frankness that is not at all disarming, that she should give up such frivolities as trying to write poetry. Romney has dedicated his life to social reform, and offers her the chance to be really useful in life by becoming his wife and helper:

> The time is done for facile settings up
> Of minnow gods, nymphs here and tritons there.   (II, 150)

Ruskin did not publish 'Of Queens' Gardens', his famous lecture on the position of women, until four years after *Aurora Leigh,* but this classic statement of Victorian commonplaces is central to the age. Ruskin attempts to combine 'wifely subjection' with a conception of the wife as the source of idealism and moral guidance, and wishes woman to receive an education that will fit her for her function of Praise, and of guarding the home from danger and temptation; she ought therefore 'to

know whatever her husband is likely to know, but to know it in a dif-
ferent way.

> . . . Speaking broadly, a man ought to know any language or science he
> learns thoroughly – while a woman ought to know it only so far as may
> enable her to sympathise in her husband's pleasures, and in those of his
> best friends.'

Romney is totally Ruskinian, advancing a view that both elevates
woman to being a moral trustee, and refuses to allow her an independent
life; and Aurora fiercely rejects this:

> am I proved too weak
> To stand alone, yet strong enough to bear
> Such leaners on my shoulder? poor to think
> Yet rich enough to sympathise with thought?   (II, 359)

She bases her rejection on the gender-neutrality of 'vocation'. A
woman dedicated to her writing – as, in later times, a woman dedicated
to any career – will give it the top priority in her life. No-one would
expect Romney to drop his vocation in order to devote himself to
marriage, and so no-one should expect it of Aurora either.

Or should they? If love is the central experience in a woman's life, it
may demand sacrifice; and the poem, to be convincing, must show that
it really is love. So the poem takes very seriously the task of showing this:
the text is conscientiously packed with hints that Aurora is in love with
Romney, beginning with the very emphatic insistence by the aunt, when
she is told what has happened:

> Yet, foolish Sweet,
> You love this man. I've watched you when he came,
> And when he went, and when we've talked of him:
> I am not old for nothing: I can tell
> The weather signs of love: you love this man.   (II, 687)

Such 'weather-signs' grow more frequent as we near the end: the way
Aurora's eyes 'leap up' when Lady Waldemar calls on her and mentions
Romney (III, 398); or her decision not to tell Romney about Lady
Waldemar's presumed treachery to Marian because she thinks they are
already married, and she will not 'agonise the man I love – I mean / The
friend I love . . . as friends love' (VII, 172). Since the poem is in the first

181

person they must, almost to the end, be no more than hints, and so are easily overinterpreted by the conventional reader, impatient for the happy ending. How are we, for instance, to regard her assertion 'I think I loved him not – nor then, nor since, Nor ever'? Is she protesting too much? Does No mean Yes? The claim that Yes means yes and No means no has become a slogan of the women's movement; but an insistence designed to prevent date rape may not be the best instrument for psychological probing. Yet such probing need not be naïvely psycho-analytic either, seeing denial always as a cover-up for assent. Such weather-signs are necessarily ambiguous, and the aunt's reading is after all only the aunt's.

There is no avoiding the fact that if Aurora is really in love with Romney, her splendid rejection of his proposal will have to be rescinded. It was the young and untried Aurora who refused; but in Book IX she takes it all back. 'Art is much,' she now declares, 'but love is more', and then, repeating the thought, promotes Love to a capital letter. The recantation is explicit and thorough: 'Romney, O my love, I am changed since then, changed wholly' (IX, 672). And the new, changed Aurora is prepared to dismiss the old fiery Aurora who

> would not be a woman like the rest,
> A simple woman who believes in love,
> And owns the right of love because she loves,
> And, hearing she's beloved, is satisfied
> With what contents God.   (IX, 660)

The passion of the earlier Aurora derived precisely from her dissatisfaction with what was offered; now, reformed, she declines into Ruskinesque contentment.

Alison Case, in an interesting study, points out that this question is involved with the technical question of point of view: are we being told the story by the young Aurora as it happens, or by the mature Aurora, which imposes a 'pattern of making the end point a center of value from which all previous positions are seen as error'? Case reports that the issue troubled at least one contemporary reviewer, who wrote: 'It is difficult to conjecture at what epoch of the story the book purports to have been written', and she goes on to claim, quite rightly, that this must not be seen as authorial carelessness, but as an expression of the conflict between romance and vocation. The apparent inconsistencies can be seen in technical terms, as they so admirably are by Case, or can be resolved by the victory of one principle over the other, as both the conventional

Victorian reader, on the one hand, and the modern feminist reader, on the other, will be tempted to do. But the only way to remain wholly true to the poem is to retain the contradiction, as Case rightly concludes: 'The contradiction between Aurora's initial "I loved him not nor then, nor since, nor ever" and her later "I loved you always" remains as unsettling to modern feminist readers as it was to that early reviewer, for it points to a deeper contradiction.'

When Aurora summarises Romney's view of marriage with the remark 'Anything does for a wife' she is rejecting Ruskin: her pithy scorn demolishes his ponderous rhetoric in a moment of truth:

> You misconceive the question like a man,
> Who sees a woman as the complement
> Of his sex merely.   (II, 434)

Even the comma in this sentence is important. 'A man who misconceives' would be a defining relative clause, implying a contrast with the man who does not misconceive the question, and so would be a rebuke addressed specifically to Romney. 'A man, who misconceives . . . ' is a descriptive or non-defining clause, lumping Romney with all other men, and adding the observation that men (of course) misconceive the question.

Aurora's Poetry

Only after the clash between the love and the vocation has been established does the poem turn to Aurora's poetic career, and enable us to ask what sort of poetry she writes:

> . . . it fluttered from my hands
> As forest leaves, stripped suddenly and rapt
> By a whirlwind on Valdarno, drop again,
> Drop slow, and strew the melancholy ground
> Before the amazéd hills . . . why so, indeed,
> I'm writing like a poet, somewhat large
> In the type of the image, and exaggerate
> A small thing with a great thing . . .   (II, 1164)

'I'm writing like a poet': that is, she cannot describe an everyday action (in this case, tearing up a document) without seizing the opportunity to compare it with something larger, to 'exaggerate / Small things

183

with a great thing.' In what sense are the forest leaves in Valdarno a 'great thing'? Perhaps because they are part of nature, so that her ordinary human action is made to seem the product of vast natural forces. Perhaps too because the image recalls Italy, the cultural beacon that always looms for Aurora, the land that drew English poets from Milton to Shelley – and, later, the Brownings.

'I'm writing like a poet': that is, too, she is self-conscious about the way she writes, and draws our attention to it. A narrative poem in which the protagonist is a poet must inevitably be self-conscious: it will contain both the poetry that the heroine writes and an awareness of what kind of poetry it is – and of the process of writing it. As we have already seen, there is a good deal of nature poetry in Aurora Leigh; and there is also a self-interrogation about writing nature poetry. Book V opens with a richly sensuous account of days

> That scarce dare breathe, they are so beautiful.
> With Spring's delicious trouble in the ground,
> Tormented by the quickened blood of roots . . .   (V, 7)

– and then goes on to ask

>   can I speak my verse
> So plainly in tune to these things and the rest,
> That men shall feel it catch them on the quick,
> As having the same warrant over them
> To hold and move them if they will or no,
> Alike imperious as the primal rhythm . . .   (V, 24)

Here too, just as much as in the question of gender and its functions, there will be a contrast between the contemporary audience and that of today. For the Victorians, what mattered in Nature poetry was the richness of the verbal texture, the capturing in language of the processes of nature, what Wordsworth had memorably called 'the infinite variety of natural appearances' and claimed that it had been hitherto neglected by poetry, and which 19th century poetry, deriving above all from Keats and Tennyson, rendered with a fidelity and fascination never previously attained (and not, as it happens, attained by Wordsworth). For today's reader, influenced by modernism and post-modernism, aware of the sense in which poetry is always about language, about its own processes, it might be the self-consciousness that is valued. For the reader of 1856 a line like 'Drop slow and strew the melancholy ground' would be of central importance, whereas 'I'm writing like a poet' would be incidental: for today's readers, this might be reversed.

This contrast is real, but, as so far stated, superficial For on the one hand the writing of descriptive poetry is not simply a matter of choosing the most accurate adjective: the very process of turning observations into language implies that perception changes the object, that the observer's awareness must form part of what is described (the plants are not articulate, it is we who bring the words). And on the other hand, a discussion of descriptive language will be abstract and barren unless it comes from a mind that knows how to describe, so that the way language involves itself with perception will not merely be gestured at from afar, but will be understood. If we ponder such a line as 'Spring's delicious trouble in the ground', we must realise, first, that it is richer and more suggestive than any more matter-of-fact account of how bulbs and seeds germinate, and second, that it is impossible to regard its two central words, 'delicious' and 'trouble', either as just about the observer's feelings or as just about what is going on under the soil. The good Victorian reader, valuing description, and the good modern reader, valuing self-awareness, will each be led towards what the other values.

It could even be claimed that the poem itself says this, in a line like 'A tree's mere firewood unless humanised' (V, 95). It then goes on to consider ways of 'humanising', beginning with the Greeks:

Which well the Greeks knew when they stirred its bark
With close-pressed bosoms of subsiding nymphs,
And made the forest-rivers garrulous
With babble of gods.   (V, 97)

Wordsworth and Coleridge were patronising to Greek mythology, which they considered a product of fancy not imagination, a substitute for direct imaginative apprehension of nature:

The Greeks in their religious poems address always the
Numina Loci, the Genii, the Dryads, the Naiads, &c, &c – All
natural Objects were dead – mere hollow Statues – but there
was a Godkin or Goddessling included in each . . . This poor
stuff . . . at best is but Fancy, or the aggregating Faculty of
the mind – not Imagination, or the modifying, and
co-adunating Faculty.

Elizabeth Browning shares such condescension, as is clear from 'garrulous'. So her lines go on to say 'For us, we are called to mark A still more intimate humanity', setting forth a doctrine of correspondences, just the doctrine expounded in one of Baudelaire's most famous poems ('La nature est un temple . . . '), a poem more or less contemporary with *Aurora Leigh,* though the doctrine is much older – Baudelaire got it from Swedenborg, but it was a commonplace of Renaissance poetry, often with references to Plato, or learned commentaries on Scripture. But what of the reader without learning? Elizabeth Browning was a learned poet writing in a more democratic age, when readers of poetry might lack a classical education. Do the best poems need to tell us about Greek mythology? What of the poet – and the reader – who cannot afford to travel to Italy to see the forest leaves in Valdarno or Vallombrosa?

Alton Locke, the eponymous hero of Kingsley's novel, sings the praises of Tennyson for a reason that may strike us, today, as odd: he calls him a democratic poet, because of 'his handling of the trivial everyday sights and sounds of nature.'

> Brought up, as I understand, in a part of England which possesses not much of the picturesque, and nothing of that which the vulgar call sublime, he has learnt to see that in all nature, in the hedgerow and the sandbank . . . is a world of true sublimity . . . I always knew there was something beautiful, wonderful, sublime, in those flowery dykes of Battersea Fields . . . and here was a man who had put them into words for me.

This can be matched in Aurora Leigh: before we are told about her actual poems, we are given an introductory account of how she sits at work watching the sun 'On lurid morns or monstrous afternoons.' It is a landscape of urban fog, and the imagery in which it is described is gruesome and astonishing:

>   – and watched the sun
> On lurid morns and monstrous afternoons
> (Like some Druidic idol's fiery brass
> With fixed unflickering outline of dead heat,
> From which the blood of wretches pent inside
> Seems oozing forth to incarnadine the air)
> Push out through fog with his dilated disk
> And startle the slant roofs and chimney pots
> With splashes of fierce colour . . .   (III, 175)

This lurid sunlight is followed by fog ('the great tawny weltering fog'), which 'wipes out London', and then by the assertion that this scene is more inspiring to poets than any 'mountains of the south' such as Sinai or Parnassus. The passage is not offered as an extract from Aurora's published work, but how much more interesting it is than the more conventional sounding poems out of which her career is built. Alton Locke would certainly have considered it democratic – though the Druids might have given him pause.

To the modern reader, that fog could have come from Eliot's Prufrock; and the contemporary poet whom it most suggests is – astonishingly – Baudelaire, looking out over the slant roofs and chimney pots of Paris, or oppressed by the heavy sky hanging like a lid. And of course both Eliot and Baudelaire are in a much more immediate sense democratic poets: they write about the world their readers inhabit. On this point Aurora – speaking here, we can hardly doubt, for her author – is very insistent:

> Nay if there's room for poets in this world . . .
> Their sole work is to represent the age,
> Their age, not Charlemagne's – this live, throbbing age,
> That brawls, cheats, maddens, calculates, aspires,
> And spends more passion, more heroic heat
> Betwixt the mirrors of its drawing rooms,
> Than Roland with his knights at Roncesvalles.   (V, 200)

Drawing rooms, yes, where she will meet Lady Waldemar, along with various spineless men who want to marry her; but also the garret in Paris where Marian nurses her child. Aurora was a learned poet (as after all was Tennyson) and much of her poetry meets conventional expectations; but she is democratic both in subject matter and in imagery. Democratic, and at times almost modern.

Finally, the question that may seem to some readers to have been pushed aside for too long: what does it mean to be a woman poet? I have postponed this because the poem has, in the end, so little to say about it. There is of course a great deal about being a woman, even about being a woman who tries to make a literary career for herself, but there is no real suggestion that the poetry itself will be any different from men's poetry. A powerful passage in Book V explores the emotional burden of her solitary occupation, and its special difficulty for women, whose natural impulse is to strive to achieve something great not for its own sake, but to commend themselves 'to some one friend'.

I'll have no traffic with the personal thought
In art's pure temple . . .
We'll keep our aims sublime, our eyes erect,
Although our woman-hands should shake and fail . . .   (V, 61)

'Although': the shaking woman-hands, the poet's personal emotion, now *gets in the way of* the poetry: this firmly ignores the Romantic doctrine that the quality of the poetry will spring from the emotional life of the poet who, according to Shelley, 'learn[s] in suffering' what he − or she! − 'teach[es] in song'. Aurora views art not as an expression of personality but as an escape from personality. Writing the poem may be harder for a woman, but there is no suggestion that the poem she writes will be different from men's poetry.

Aurora was obviously entitled to hold an impersonal theory of poetry; but the author was perhaps less entitled to it, since she did, after all, write *Aurora Leigh*: a work that has the complexities of a novel, and many of the impersonal qualities of an epic, but also springs out of the author's own situation as a woman writer, with an immediacy that Aurora (it appears) does not try to emulate.

Note   There are two convenient editions of *Aurora* Leigh: that in the World's Classics, edited with a good introduction by Kerry MacSweeney; and the much fuller Norton Critical Edition, which contains the text of the poem, relevant contemporary documents, and a large number of modern essays, including Alison Case's 'Gender and Narration in *Aurora Leigh*', which originally appeared in *Victorian Poetry*, vol. 29, no. 1 (Spring 1991). Milton's famous simile about Vallombrosa comes in *Paradise Lost* Book 2, line 302. Ruskin's essay on the education of women, *Of Queens' Gardens*, forms the second section of *Sesame and Lilies* (1865). Coleridge's remarks on the religious poetry of the Greeks are in a letter to William Sotheby, 10 September 1802. Baudelaire's poem that sees Nature as a temple is *Correspondances*; the description of the Parisian roofscapes is *Paysage*, that of the heavy sky hanging like a lid is *Spleen* ('Quand le ciel bas et lourd . . . '): all appeared in *Les Fleurs du Mal* (1857). The remark on Tennyson as a democratic poet occurs in Kingsley's *Alton Locke* (1850), chapter 9.

A Name of One's Own

'Chloe likes Olivia and they share a laboratory.' These eight words are perhaps the most concentrated and suggestive sentence ever written about women's literature. It takes two rather literary names and gives them to two emancipated modern young women, evidently with careers (the fact that both these names have now become quite common in our society adds a small extra irony to the sentence). The really revolutionary word in that sentence is, of course, 'likes', reminding us that literature is full of women who love and are loved, but that custom has not allowed them plain ordinary liking, or, if it has, that sentiment has not been felt as material for literature in the way the affection of Damon for Pythias or Hamlet for Horatio has been perceived as an interesting and unsexual relationship worth writing about. (Again there is a recent complication: the present popularity of gay studies invites us to find sexual elements in what was once the untroubled asexuality of same-sex friendship.)

The sentence comes, as many readers will already have recognised, from *A Room of One's Own*, surely the most influential and the most frequently cited book on women's writing. It is a book which is willing to take material conditions very seriously. It illustrates the prestige enjoyed by men's colleges and not by women's by the quality of the food they serve: 'partridges, many and various, with all their retinue of sauces and salads' at the men's college, prunes and custard at the women's (leaving feminists with the dilemma, whether to imitate or to despise such material trappings). As for the requirement for a writing woman – five hundred a year and a room of one's own – which provides the title of Woolf's book and, ignoring inflation, has passed into the language: this owes its power to the way it is poised between saying two quite different and equally necessary things: freedom from excessive sexual demands, and a place to work undisturbed. No other woman managed so brilliant an aphorism, but George Eliot came close: 'O the bliss of having a very high attic in a romantic continental town, such as Geneva – far away from morning callers, dinners and decencies' (letter to John Sibree, 14 May 1848). Here too the passage of time has added an irony: she got such a room in Geneva, and the city fathers have now decorated it with a plaque, informing the no doubt bewildered Genevois that a young English writer called 'Miss Evans' lived there.

The woman poet who embodied the demand for independence most fiercely was probably Emily Brontë, with her solitary walks and her intense need for privacy, her addressing of the god within her breast as if he dwelt within her breast and nowhere else, as if he was freed from 'the thousand creeds / that move men's hearts'. In her case independence does not even seem to have required freedom from domestic duties, which she is said to have carried out very competently, but simply the opportunity to take walks by herself, and keep her writing private – so private that her sister Charlotte, accidentally discovering a notebook of Emily's poems, had great difficulty in persuading her into joint publication (and may never have been completely forgiven for the intrusion). Emily's uncompromising independence was central to her nature, as, in its very different way, was that of the other Emily, 'the character of Amherst', who did manage to have a room of her own, and seldom went out of it; but such fierce solitariness is not standard among woman poets, as it is not among women. The counter tendency is, of course, the need for love: this has waged a constant battle with the need for independence in the breast of many (perhaps most) women – and many men too. Perhaps no woman writer illustrates the tension between these two pulls better than Charlotte Brontë: 'No young lady should fall in love,' she wrote to her friend Ellen Nussey, 'till the offer has been made, accepted – the marriage ceremony performed and the first half-year of wedded life has passed away': Jane Austen herself (who never married and published no poetry) could hardly have bettered the ironic coolness of this. We might not know how intense was Charlotte Brontë's need for love if she had never written novels: the spirited independence of Jane Eyre and Lucy Snowe yields, in the end, to an emotional intensity that seems to burst the bounds of prose (though Charlotte Brontë's poems never attain anything like the intensity of these novels).

'Five hundred a year and a room of one's own': those are the things that matter, and in comparison names are trivial – just labels. In the last act of Shaw's comedy *You Never Can Tell*, Mr Bohun, as he sorts out the complications of plot, begins with people's names. When told that the important questions should be disposed of first, he replies 'There will be no difficulty about the important questions. There never is. It's the trifles that will wreck you at the harbour mouth.' Names may be trifles, but the women's movement has shown considerable sympathy with Mr Bohun's view. Do we think of our name as a mere label, stuck on to one's outside like one's clothes, or is it somehow a part of ourself, essential to our personality (and perhaps this could be asked of our clothes too)? When Bridget Smith turns into Mrs Rochester (in earlier days, even into Mrs Edward Rochester) is this just an unimportant switch of label? (After all, the Smith she began with was just another man's name.) Or are our names part of our identity, so that to lose them is to lose something of ourselves? Today Bridget Smith might cling to a vestige of her original identity by becoming Bridget Smith Rochester. Or she might publish her poems under her maiden name, which is after all something that will not change. Given today's divorce figures, she may cease to be Rochester and become Bridget St John – perhaps (awkwardly) after she has published a book or two as Rochester.

This can be a problem for us as well as for her: by 'us' I mean the critics and biographers who write about her. The obvious enlightened policy is to let the woman herself choose, and for every woman who chooses to remain Sylvia Plath there is another who chooses to become Virginia Woolf. And for those who lived before such options were available? How do we refer to Victorian women writers? No-one has insisted on calling Mrs Humphrey Ward either 'Mary Ward' or 'Mary Arnold', or on unmarrying Edith Wharton. Of course one can drop all titles, along with Christian names, as one does with males, so that Christina Rossetti becomes 'Rossetti', and Mary Shelley becomes 'Shelley'. As it happens, Mary Shelley hasn't become 'Shelley', but Christina Rossetti has become 'Rossetti', with all the resultant confusion when she is discussed along with her brothers.

The three-name solution – Elizabeth Barrett Browning – is the most popular, especially if that is how the poet had her own name printed in her Poems. But when we drop the Christian name – as, after all, we do for men – we cannot, obviously, call her Browning, so she has become 'Barrett Browning', which has a good modern ring to it. Does it matter that she would never have dreamed of calling herself that? Or that the 'Barrett' in the middle of her threefold name is not actually her unmarried surname, but a given name, since she was actually born Elizabeth Barrett Moulton. One begins to see advantages in calling Katherine Philips 'the matchless Orinda'.

It is, of course, no use saying that none of this matters now she is dead – all the poets discussed in this book, as readers have no doubt noticed, are dead. How we form the name of a dead female poet matters not to her but to us – as indeed rescuing her poems from oblivion is something we do for ourselves. She may of course, while alive, have imagined the title she would retain after death, and even written teasingly about it.

Title divine – is mine!
The Wife – without the sign!
Acute Degree – conferred on me –
Empress of Calvary! . . .
'My Husband' – women say –
Stroking the Melody.

Stroking the melody: that is what we can do for our dead mothers; that is what this book has tried to do.

Index

Women poets discussed

Barbauld, Anna Laetitia, 38, 50
Behn, Aphra, 17
Bishop, Elizabeth, 139
Blind, Mathilde, 104
Bradstreet, Anne, 20
Brookes, Gwendolyn, 155
Brontë, Emily, 80,190
Browning, Elizabeth Barrett, 59, 68, 177, 191

Carey, Mary, 21
Chudleigh, Lady, 34
Cromwell, Elizabeth, 22

H.D. (Hilda Doolittle), 145
Dacre, Charlotte, 38, 40
Daryush, Elizabeth, 164
Dickinson, Emily, 1,111, 192

Eliot, George (Marian Evans), 86, 189

Finch, Anne, 25

Greenwell, Dora, 71

Hemans, Felicia, 55

Landon, Laetitia Elizabeth 55
Levertov, Denise, 145
Levy, Amy, 108

Mew, Charlotte, 123
Millay, Edna St Vincent, 152
Montagu, Lady Mary Wortley, 28

Moore, Marianne, 130
More, Hannah, 38, 40

Opie, Amelia, 38

Philips, Katherine, 11
Pitter, Ruth, 166

Raine, Kathleen, 168
Robinson, Mary, 46
Rossetti, Christina, 71, 91

Smith, Charlotte, 42
Smith, Stevie, 171

Thomas, Elizabeth, 34

Webster, Augusta, 77, 100
Wheatley, Phillis, 37
Williams, Helen Maria, 38
Wright, Hetty, 35

Male poets, critics and topics

Barthes, Roland, 49
Baudelaire, Charles, 107, 185
Berdoe, Edward, 65
Blackwood, John, 86
Blake, William, 48, 51
Brecht, Bert, 175
Bridges, Robert, 122, 164
Brontë, Charlotte, 80, 190
Brontë, Rev Patrick, 86
Browning, Robert, 59, 63
Byron, Lord, 64

Cartwright, William, 12
Case, Alison, 182
Cixous, Hélène, 128
Coleridge, Samuel Taylor, 52, 185
Corinne, 56

Daly, Mary, 128
Denman, Kamilla, 119
De Stael, Mme, 56
Donne, John, 1, 15
Dryden, John, 2
Du Bartas, G, 20

Earle, Marian, 72

Fletcher, John, 147
Franklin, R.W., 118

Gide, André, 110
Greer, Germaine, 4

Hardy, Thomas, 70, 124
Heine, Heinrich, 175
Herrick, Robert, 23
Higginson, T. W., 112, 122
Hood, Thomas, 70
Hopkins, G. M., 120
Housman, A. E., 99

Johnson, Thomas H., 118
Jonson, Ben, 15

Keats, John, 12, 88, 135, 169
King Lear, 27,72
Kirkup, James, 168

Leighton, Angela, 102
Lister, T. H., 3

Mallarmé, S, 110
McGann, Jerome, 99
Metre and rhyme, 133, 149

Milton, John, 106
Monro, Harold, 124
Munby, Arthur, 69

Nevinson, H.W., 126

Ostriker, Alicia, 154

Pacheco, Anita, 7
Pindaric Ode, 25
Pope, Alexander, 30
Priestley, Joseph, 53

Ransom, John Crowe, 118
Rich, Adrienne, 118
Rossetti, Dante Gabriel, 70
Ruskin, John, 62, 180

Sappho, 56
Selden, R., 8
Shaw, George Bernard, 190
Shakespeare, William, 98
Sims, George R., 70
Slavery, 37
Sterne, Laurence, 41
Stevens, Wallace, 90
Stevenson, Anne, 144
Suckling, Sir John, 153

Tanner, Sarah, 69
Taylor, Jeremy, 13
Tennyson, Alfred, 94, 100
Thomson, James, 108
Todd, Mabel Loomis, 111

Villanelle, 143

Woolf, Virginia, 189
Wordsworth, William, 4, 9, 43, 44,
    107, 178, 184, 185

Yonge, Mrs, 29